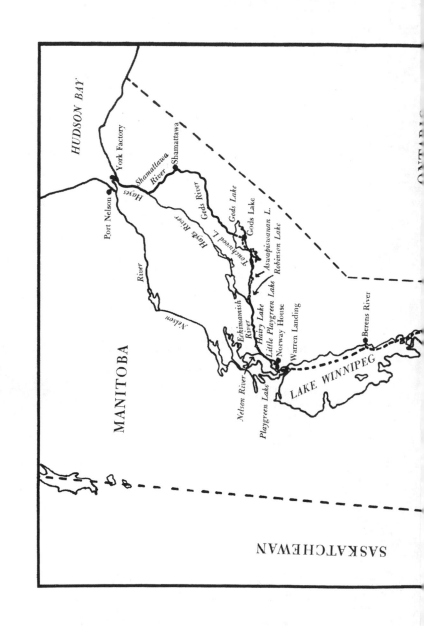

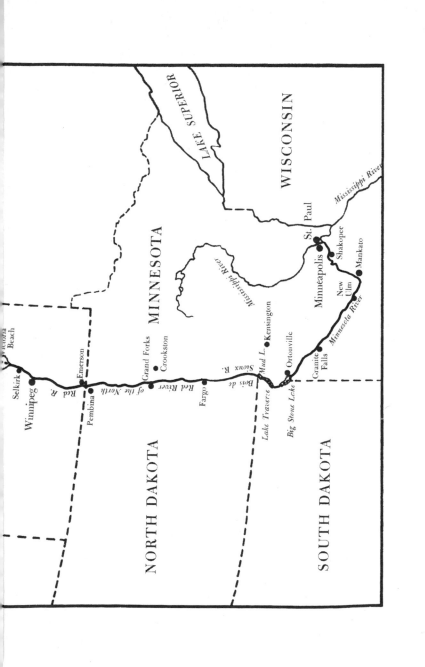

LAKE SUPERIOR

WISCONSIN

MINNESOTA

St. Paul

Shakopee

Minneapolis

New Ulm

Mankato

Mississippi River

Mississippi River

Minnesota River

Kensington

Mud L.

Ortonville

Granite Falls

Victoria Beach

Emerson

Grand Forks

Crookston

Sioux R.

Lake Traverse

Bois de

Big Stone Lake

Selkirk

Red R.

Red River of the North

Fargo

Winnipeg

Pembina

NORTH DAKOTA

SOUTH DAKOTA

# CANOEING WITH THE CREE

# CANOEING
## *with the* CREE

*by*
## ERIC SEVAREID

*Foreword by*
## Ann Bancroft

**BOREALIS**
**BOOKS**

Borealis Books is an imprint of the Minnesota Historical Society Press.

www.borealisbooks.org

The Minnesota Historical Society Press is a
member of the Association of American University Presses.

Manufactured in the United States of America

10 9 8 7 6 5 4 3

∞ The paper used in this publication meets the minimum requirements of the American National Standard for Information Sciences—Permanence for Printed Library Materials, ANSI Z39.48-1984.

International Standard Book Number
ISBN 13: 978-0-87351-533-7 (paper)
ISBN 10: 0-87351-533-1 (paper)

*Library of Congress Cataloging-in-Publication Data*

Sevareid, Eric, 1912–
    Canoeing with the Cree / Eric Sevareid ; foreword by Ann Bancroft.
        p. cm.
    Includes index.
    ISBN 0-87351-533-1 (pbk. : alk. paper)
    1. Sevareid, Eric, 1912– —Travel.
    2. Sevareid, Eric, 1912– —Childhood and youth.
    3. Canoes and canoeing.
    4. Cree Indians.
    I. Title.
    GV782.42.S48A3 2004
    797.122—dc22

                                                      2004026307

Printed by Thomson-Shore, Inc., Dexter, Michigan, on Glatfelter Natures, a sheet made completely from recycled paper, including fifty percent post-consumer waste.

# FOREWORD

Just a few miles from the spot where *Canoeing with the Cree* begins, and forty years later, I put in on my first Mississippi River canoe trip. Stories of adventure had captivated me for as long as my mother remembers, and several summers earlier, at Camp Widjiwagan, I had been smitten with love for canoes. My dad gave me a copy of *Canoeing*, which I remember relishing.

It was April when my dad, my brother Hunter, and I set out for several days on the river, which was swollen with spring snowmelt and rain. We put in near our house in Mendota and were due back home several days later in time for my older brother Bill's birthday. A call to my mom at trip's end would summon our pick-up. But we were late, wind-bound and trapped on a muddy island overnight. A search team of tugboats panning the shore with huge spotlights couldn't find us, nor did it occur to us that the light show was on our behalf. The size and challenge of the "mighty" river were legendary in our minds, so we simply resigned ourselves to being among the many who would sleep on its shore and live to tell a story.

*Canoeing with the Cree,* this remarkable account by two young men about to graduate from high school, begins as do many youthful dreams. On the cusp of adulthood, with nothing ostensible to lose, Eric Sevareid and his friend Walt Port decide to leave the comforts of their homes to seek adventure—in a secondhand, eighteen-foot, voyageur-style canoe. While Minneapolis was already a mature city in 1930, the wilderness of the great north woods was as close as a train stop, or two, away. Early in the boys' trip, just a few hundred into the eventual 2,500 miles, they look out over the Minnesota River from a tower at Fort Ridgely. From this high vantage Sevareid muses that there is much more river ahead! Their long trek north along many rivers, passing early trading posts and eventually reaching the great Hudson Bay and sea beyond, would be the first documented canoe trip along this historic route. There is no question but that the naiveté of youth and the strength of both young men's characters made fate favor their success.

The *Minneapolis Star* newspaper, the canoe journey's only sponsor, first published *Canoeing with the Cree* in 1935. It is based on Sevareid's journal notes and a series of newspaper stories filed en route, for which the duo was paid the sum of $100 in two $50 installments. The articles brought home to enthusiastic readers the young explorers' world of muskeg, searing heat, constant unknown, and unfamiliar cultural encounters. As wilderness diminishes in our own time, having been reduced to a concept, and a memory, by our insatiable spread over the land, this elegant recounting of a historic trip is still one of the best adventure stories in my library.

The long and productive lives of each hero, Eric Sevareid, a renowned journalist, and Walter Port, his compatriot, give readers a comfortable viewpoint from which to measure the real risks and near-death experiences of canoeing north from Fort Snelling to Hudson Bay in 1930. In the way that one can hire a Twin Otter plane to fly a party to the North Pole today, an explorer's journal allows us to share the experience from a comfortable armchair but skip the planning, preparation, and physical rigors of the trip itself. Although the written record cannot substitute for the real experience, readers gain an appreciation for history and the value of wilderness travel itself from reading detailed personal chronicles. I have visualized many of my own trips this way by first reading earlier accounts.

Among the themes that resound in Sevareid's book, the most palpable for me is the power of language and storytelling. With almost no access to the communication wires necessary to send out their stories, the explorer-writers had to thread their news together with great gaps in time and without visuals in order for their readers to "see" and feel their experiences. This also worked to captivate their audience, bringing attention to their efforts and challenging their doubters. In 1930 one waited for news—and waited as long as necessary. The isolation of eastern Manitoba presented readers a contrasting world of indigenous cultures and backcountry men living a largely physical lifestyle that set the stage for a heroic saga. Is it only coincidence that short attention spans and the loss of wilderness characterize our time? We may need to rely on stories such as this one to remind us of what wind in the tree tops sounded like without the roar of a nearby freeway. Readers can imagine the hushed sounds of the native Cree language, the feel of rabbit-fur moccasin liners, the scent of native white pine forests, and the distant whistle of "iron" foreshadowing a noisier, more time-pressed day.

Borealis Books' reissue of *Canoeing with the Cree* is an important statement on behalf of great books. This is a gem, and its relevance today is unquestionable. We in the outdoor community face a tremendous challenge: We must persuade others to preserve wilderness not just to protect the planet's biodiversity, but because wilderness is essential to our spiritual well-being.

I write about my travels to remote places to remind my friends of the importance of preserving wilderness, knowing that this is a bit of a paradox. How will we shape our worldview without a fundamental understanding of our struggle to live vividly as human organisms? The wilderness experience, as Sevareid shows, positions the great questions we face in life within the context of our utter smallness. Only our acceptance, our willingness to go where we are small and where we need to respect the power and objectivity of nature, makes it possible for us to experience a hero's journey. And we are all eager for that journey.

ANN BANCROFT

# FOREWORD TO THE ORIGINAL EDITION

THIS book tells the story of the unusual experience of two boys who not only proved that youth and determination can accomplish what older men often fail at, but who demonstrated something else that is very significant.

They demonstrated in their amazing journey that the spirit of personal adventure is not yet dead, that opportunities for adventurous living have not yet disappeared.

It refreshes me to think of that, and it must be doubly refreshing and encouraging to the young boys and girls of America, who sense that the days of frontier living, with their adventures, are gone.

The boys in this story have shown the contrary; they have demonstrated that the frontiers—the frontiers of courage and romance, still exist, beyond which only the exceptional soul will venture. One has only to choose a setting for the drama; they chose theirs in a wild, untamed land. Yours may be in your home surrounding, but if your mind is an imaginative one, if your heart seeks the unexplored, the setting does not matter. Your life will be an adventure.

GEORGE H. ADAMS.

Editor, *The Minneapolis Star,*
Minneapolis, Minnesota, 1935

# CONTENTS

PAGE

CHAPTER

I. WE'RE OFF!     1

II. THE NEW LIFE     10

III. SNAKES!     26

IV. TRAGEDY—ALMOST     41

V. RED RIVER MUD     53

VI. READY FOR THE PLUNGE     64

VII. INTO THE LAND OF THE CREE     78

VIII. THE ROYAL NORTHWEST MOUNTED     91

IX. HUMILIATION OF THE "SANS SOUCI"     104

X. "THE DIE IS CAST"     114

XI. CANOEING WITH THE CREE     128

XII. GOD'S COUNTRY     141

XIII. THE GREAT TEST     153

XIV. VICTORY—AND PINEAPPLE     172

XV. HALF-BREEDS AND MUSKEG     185

XVI. END OF THE TRAIL     198

INDEX     202

# ILLUSTRATIONS

*facing page*

Arnold E. Sevareid.   14

Walter C. Port.   14

Walt dragging the canoe through a shallow stretch in the Minnesota River.   15

A victim of Red River mud.   15

The *Sans Souci* lodged in the narrowest part of the Minnesota—a half mile from source.   32

Walt rescues a mired lamb.   33

Blue heron on Minnesota River.   33

Indian settlement on lower Lake Winnipeg.   92

Where the Red River empties into Lake Winnipeg.   92

Hudson Bay buildings at Berens River. Lake Winnipeg in background.   93

Air view of Warren's Landing, north end of Lake Winnipeg.   93

Air view of fort at Norway House—where we began our 500 mile wilderness jump.   116

A glimpse of God's Lake and the many islands.   116

Camp at evening. Bud dries out the fishing line.   117

The start of a fishing trip at God's Lake.   117

Bud essays a difficult portage with pack held by tump-line.   134

Lunch with our Indian companions. Moses and Jimmy in the center, Walt at right, washing dishes.   135

# ILLUSTRATIONS

*facing page*

Pow-is-tick Rapids on the Nelson River, north of Norway House, which we avoided by our route to the Bay.     135

Part of the Indian settlement at God's Lake.     146

Trading post at God's Lake. Left to right—Butchart, Barton, Solomon, Henry, and Indians.     146

A Cree boy demonstrates for us with his bow and arrow.     147

Typical Indian scene at God's Lake.     147

Falls on God's River which we did *not* run. Wonderful trout fishing here.     160

One of the many rapids on God's River which we *did* run.     160

Walt with grub box on top of the load; starts a portage on God's River.     161

Halfbreeds all dressed up for Sunday at the corrugated tin church at York Factory.     161

Unloading the schooner *Fort York* at York Factory.     180

The great Shamattawa rapid, two miles long, which we ran on the wrong side. 100 miles from Hudson Bay.     180

Air view of York Factory where our journey ended.     181

Last resting place of the *Sans Souci*. Our canoe lies face down, on the exact spot we landed.     181

CANOEING WITH THE CREE

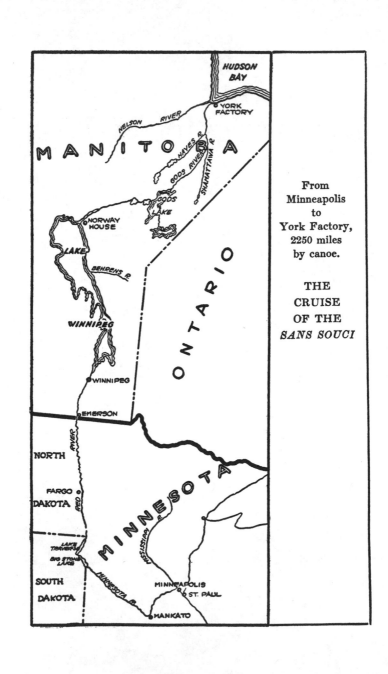

HUDSON
BAY

NELSON RIVER

YORK
FACTORY

M A N I T O B A

HAYES R.

GODS RIVER

SHAMATTAWA R.

GODS
LAKE

NORWAY
HOUSE

LAKE

BEHRENS R.

O N T A R I O

WINNIPEG

WINNIPEG

EMERSON

NORTH

RED RIVER

FARGO

DAKOTA

M I N N E S O T A

MISSISSIPPI R.

LAKE
TRAVERSE

BIG STONE
LAKE

SOUTH

DAKOTA

MINNESOTA R.

MINNEAPOLIS
ST. PAUL

MANKATO

From
Minneapolis
to
York Factory,
2250 miles
by canoe.

THE
CRUISE
OF THE
*SANS SOUCI*

## CHAPTER I

# WE'RE OFF!

*"Now the Four Way Lodge is opened, now the Hunting
  Winds are loose,
Now the Smokes of Spring go up to clear the brain;
Now the Young Men's hearts are troubled for the whisper
  of the Trues;
Now the Red Gods make their medicine again. . . .
We must go, go, go away from here.
On the other side the world we're overdue. . . ."*

IT was a warm May afternoon, and my class
in English literature was almost ended when I
happened to turn to that page of Kipling. The
sunshine was streaming in the room, shining on a
bent-over head of light hair in front of me and
falling in funny speckles on the book page. As
the spots of light shifted back and forth over the
type, it seemed as though the letters were alive
and crawling in bewilderment, trying to get
away.

I watched them curiously for a while, and the

1

lines of the verse I had just read kept sounding in my brain over and over again. I heard nothing else until the teacher said, in a loud voice that made the letters suddenly stop their movement:

"Tomorrow it will be *Paradise Lost.*"

That completely awakened me and I had an overwhelming sense that everything was wrong. *Paradise Lost,* indeed! As long as I remained in that suddenly confining room, I knew it was lost. Paradise was outdoors, out on the greening hills and along the lazy river.

I could see that Walt was thinking hard of something too, for he seemed to be staring at the window, looking right through the file of students who were walking from the room. In a minute it was quiet and he and I were alone.

He got up slowly, walked over by me and slumped down in the next seat. As he screwed up his fountain pen he said: "Bud, why in the world don't we get out of here this summer—go somewhere. I'd be partial to the North Pole or South Africa, myself."

So that is how it all started. Mr. Kipling made the first move, but I guess Walt Port will have to get most of the credit—or the blame. It

2

wasn't South Africa or the North Pole we headed for, but it was well on the way toward the latter. It was Hudson Bay.

Walt really had kept a plan for the trip a secret with himself all through high school, waiting until graduation to spring it.

Briefly, it was this:

We would paddle a canoe up the Minnesota River from Minneapolis, our home, to Big Stone Lake, on the South Dakota line, into the Red River of the North, down that river into Canada and Lake Winnipeg, up the east shore of the lake to Norway House and, at that point, attempt a hazardous wilderness jump of five hundred miles to the bay. It would be the first time an all-water trip had ever been made from Minnesota to the North Atlantic ocean.

Marvelous! It sounded so simple then. But the problems in the way were many, and the first was finances.

"I've an answer to that," I announced after a few moments' heavy thought. "Why not get one of the newspapers in town to finance us? We could write weekly stories for them about our progress." (I was editor of the school paper and considered myself a second Robert Louis Stevenson.)

"Bud," Walt said with admiration, "for once in your spotted career you have an idea. Do you think we can put it over?"

One newspaper did turn us down. Impossible, they told us, for two high-school kids, one nineteen (Walt) and the other seventeen (me) to make a trip like that. Grown men would fail at it. Besides, our stories probably would not be any good, anyway.

But Mr. W. C. Robertson, managing editor of the *Minneapolis Star,* thought differently. Or at least he did after we had harried him for a week.

One day he called us down to his office. "All right, boys, we'll ride with you," he announced briefly.

Stopping only long enough to thank him with a gasp, we tore out of the newspaper building for the nearest camping-goods store to begin selecting our outfit. Never, never had we been so excited! People stopped to stare at the two of us, one long and lean, the other short and stocky, galloping through the streets, talking as

4

fast as we could with both our mouths and all our hands.

Considering our inexperience, we finally selected a fairly compact and durable outfit. Our canoe was eighteen feet long, an American-made cruiser model, with a wide beam and a small keel. Some canoeists argued against the use of a keel, but later on we were thankful we had one.

The *Sans Souci,* we christened her. That was Walt's idea. It means "without care." We painted on her, "Minneapolis to Hudson Bay." In order to beat other buyers for the canoe, which was secondhand and on which the middle thwart was missing, we had to skip some of our final examinations.

One necessary item we deliberately neglected to secure until we were assured of the *Star's* backing was the consent of our folks, who were caused more worry the ensuing summer than the hides of Walt and me were worth. But when they saw we had everything figured out almost to the last detail, they said "yes" like good sports. Both our dads wished they could go too.

It really was a wonder they let us go. Some

of our teachers at school called them and insisted that we would surely get lost in the wilderness, that we would drown, or that we would be wrecked in the rapids. A college professor who was planning to go up in the north country on a scientific expedition the next spring offered to take us along if we would give up this trip, and said that we never could hear the waterfalls until it was too late. And the football coach, who wanted us to save money so we could go to college the next fall, argued with us for several hours.

But our minds were made up. I suppose people try to discourage everyone who starts a trip like ours. You just have to make up your minds you can do it and then go ahead.

The principal of the school thought it was great. He announced it at a student-council meeting and said it was "the nearest thing to the Lewis and Clark Expedition he had ever heard of."

Commencement night finally rolled around. Here were our classmates, all around us, faces shining, proud as peacocks, and there were our teachers and folks beyond the footlights. My

6

heart tugged a little at the thought of leaving them all so soon. Would we see them again?

Walt was president of our class, by right of general admiration, although he always said it was my political maneuvering. He led the march for the diplomas and awkwardly turned the wrong way, leading the whole class off the stage at the wrong exit. I'm afraid Walt wasn't thinking of diplomas that night. He was thinking of Indians and rapids and Mounted Police.

Walt came to stay at our house the night before we set out. We sat around the fireplace for a long time, talking excitedly, until finally father chased us up to bed, fearful that we would be too tired for our first day's travel. But I could not sleep much.

Early light was beginning to show the things in my room—my typewriter, my old easy chair, and my books on the desk—when I opened my eyes on that day we started out. Then I think I realized, fully and clearly for the first time, the immensity of the thing we were about to attempt. I went cold to the pit of my stomach, but just for an instant. Walt stirred, grunted and sat up, and I had other things to think about.

I suppose it was harder for our folks to say good-by than for us. They must do all the worrying and wondering about our safety. It is always easier when you are doing the thing yourself.

It was June seventeenth. Finally we pushed off into the Mississippi, rode the fast current down a mile and turned into the channel of the Minnesota River, which empties into the Mississippi at Minneapolis.

We started out on the trip with the following equipment:

eighteen-foot canoe
three five-foot, c o p p e r - tipped paddles
two sponges for canoe cleaning
pack sack with food in small canvas bags
pack sack with clothes and miscellaneous articles
four wool blankets rolled in two rubber ponchos
gunny sack with cooking utensils
one army pup tent
.22 caliber rifle, single shot

all-purpose pocket knife
skinning knife in sheath
heavy hatchet in sheath
pocket whetstone
bottle of boot oil
bottle of mosquito lotion
length of mosquito netting
diary book
waterproof match container
one-gallon water bag
one tin pail
rod and reel
smoked glasses
length of small rope
personal toilet articles

8

## WE'RE OFF!

first-aid kit
travelers' checks, five dollars in cash
closely cropped hair
carefully examined teeth
camera, films
maps, army compass
cooking grate
can of canoe tar
high boots
many pairs of wool socks
breeches, plus long trousers
wool shirt, cotton shirt apiece
heavy wool underwear for sleeping
heavy sweater apiece (excellent as pillows)
swimming suits
felt hats with wide brims
frying pan
two small kettles with loop handles
two tin cups
three pie tins for plates
tablespoons, not teaspoons
steel wool to clean pans

## For food supply we had:

one small ham
side of bacon
pound of tea
two pounds sugar
half-pound salt
ten pounds rice
peanut butter
pound of flour for frying fish
bread
three pounds raisins
three pounds prunes
potatoes
several cans of beans
supply of uncooked beans
several cans of prepared soups
sweet chocolate

## CHAPTER II

## *THE NEW LIFE*

WE were off! The trail stretched ahead, a twisting stream of gleaming green water. As we began to paddle against the stiff current, we could hear a bugle playing and the guns firing at Fort Snelling. Overhead several airplanes were circling—not in our honor, for our start was very inauspicious, but the unintentional salutations were timely.

At the first bend I turned and looked back. Our families were still on the dock, watching. A few more strokes of our paddles and green willows slid out and hid the dock. We were alone with the green water, the mossy banks, and the trees which bent over the edge.

Walter and I had lots of ideas about how we would work things. We decided at the start to get up every morning at five o'clock, take an hour's rest at noon and paddle until five in the evening, which would give us about ten hours of paddling a day. But there is no use in making many schedules while you are out in the woods, for things seldom happen in regular fashion.

The first day we learned a little about paddling in time with each other, using a short, powerful stroke. We made one plan at least which we did stick to. We decided that one of us would take the stern and the other the bow each noon and the next noon we would change about.

We worked out a system for getting tanned also, for it was very hot on the river, and for the first few days our faces and hands were blistered raw. We would take off our shirts for five minutes for a few days and increase the time by five minutes each day after that. Later, on Lake Winnipeg, when the days were cool and no one was about, we traveled simply in white trunks.

"Always camp by a spring of water," the woodcraft books read, and that's what we tried to do that first night. Drainage ditches and sewers confused us for a long time, but finally we found an honest-to-goodness spring of fresh water, and following book rules we camped there, even if the spot was not very good. Later on we simply filled our water bag from some farmer's pump and camped wherever we pleased.

Walt was elected official cook that first night and his cooking, if I may call it that, resulted in shriveled chunks of ham resembling cinders. Raw prunes and tea completed the meal.

If I ever make another long trip, I will not take an army pup tent. The obstinate piece of canvas got more out of shape and more difficult to erect every night, and it was a blessing when we could discard it.

How much easier it is to sit in a chair at home and read about "the things to do when camping." Things look so easy in print, but when the tent won't go up, when the beans tip in the fire, when the water won't boil and when it suddenly begins to rain in the midst of supper, then all the directions in the world won't help and it's every man to his own method. For Walter and I, when we started out, knew practically nothing of woods life. Never before had we really traveled by canoe. So everything we learned at first hand and many were the scars, burns, cold meals and miserable nights that accumulated before all the lessons were learned.

We draped several yards of netting over the tent entrance and blocked up the sides with our clothes—but try to keep mosquitoes out when they are determined to get in! One of the reasons we were bitten so freely was my pair of feet. They are too far from my head, and more than once I kicked out the netting.

Walt still insists he slept well the first night on the trail. I admit without shame that I did not. The ground seemed awfully hard. We used four blankets, spread between two ponchos, rubber sheets that protected us from the damp ground and which kept our blankets dry when we did not use the tent. So our arrangement amounted practically to a large sleeping bag.

Everything was damp the next morning, including our spirits, for a heavy fog had descended and soaked all our equipment. Thereafter, we kept the packs covered with our slickers. I cooked pancakes for our first breakfast and, but for the fact that they were burned on the outside and doughy inside, they were good. We began immediately the practice of using sand and grass to

13

wash our dishes, for they are about the only things that will take grease out of a frying pan. We had stomach aches and no appetites for a week, which seemed strange, because always before we had eaten ravenously when in the woods. This was due, of course, to the intense heat and to our own bad cooking.

We were aiming for Hudson Bay, which is straight north of Minneapolis, but the first six days we paddled directly south to Mankato, twenty-five miles from the Iowa border. At this point the Minnesota River bends to the west and north.

Near the little town of Carver, we met our first little stretch of fast water. It was a tiny rapid compared to those we later encountered, but we were very excited and paddled and poled furiously to get up through it.

At Shakopee we bought a copy of the *Star* and there, right on the front page, were our pictures and a long story about the trip. They said it was "daring." I guess it made us both think the same thing—"We've got to do it now."

Although the fish in the Minnesota River are mostly carp, a rough fish, we saw fishermen every

Arnold E. Sevareid.

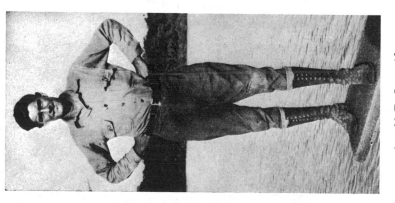

Walter C. Port.

Walt dragging the canoe through a shallow stretch in the
Minnesota River.

A victim of Red River mud.

day, but never witnessed a catch. One fisherman, near Shakopee, a town named for the "terrible Shakopee," a Sioux who massacred many whites in the great uprising of 1862, told us we would never get even as far as Mankato, because there were too many sand bars and the current was too strong. He expressed the sentiment of almost everyone we met. It was surprising, and a bit discouraging, too, that so few people thought we could get to the bay.

One old farmer near Mankato said to me, "Hudson Bay? Why, it will be snowing before you can get into Canada." Soon after that, a boy swimming in the river, noticing the sign on our boat, shouted, "Betcha two bits you don't get there!" Three weeks later as we were passing between the two Lake Traverses, two men got out of their car on a bridge and yelled: "Are you the two —— fools from Minneapolis?"

Cheering folks!

Many times we wished we could have afforded a moving-picture camera. We did have Walt's kodak, however, and although we could not spend much for films, we took a good number of pictures. One exceptional shot, which was printed in many newspapers, was of a big blue heron. The poor bird was crippled and, by a little chasing up the shore and down again, we snapped it standing in shallow water.

Once, while crossing Lake Traverse, after a long chase we got a picture of a wild pelican, the first we had ever seen, but the picture was lost somehow.

Above one stretch of rapids, Walt and I both got out and hiked to a farm for some water. We had stuck a paddle through a loop in the canoe chain and sunk it in the mud, but when we returned to the river our canoe was gone.

Frantically we strained our eyes everywhere. Then we saw it. The *Sans Souci* was calmly drifting under an arbor of bending willows, innocently moving toward the rocks and fast water. Once in the fast water, she might be smashed or upset and our outfit lost. Desperately we raced along the shore, cursing savagely the mud that sucked at our boots. Just in time, we caught her as her speed was quickening for the slide into the rocks. After that, when we left her, we tied the canoe tightly enough to hold a rogue elephant.

Hailing people along the banks, we always

16

asked the distances between towns and sought information about the river ahead. We learned, after a time, not to believe anything in the matter of distance. One man would say it was ten miles to the next village and another man, around the next bend, would say it was fifteen miles. So we figured it out ourselves from our map and from what we knew of the river's ways.

Near the village of Henderson, after a long boring afternoon, we came across a small mud flat, where carp were swimming in the shallow water. Eager for sport, we climbed out and chased them up and down with our paddles. We nearly broke the paddles and splashed a lot of mud in each other's faces, but didn't come near one of the fish.

That afternoon we waded across a sand bar, dragging the canoe, and for the next week we were doing it several times a day. Of course, we kept our boots well oiled. We had one try at camping on sand bars—and never again! Sleeping on the soft sand was great, but the whole outfit was full of the stuff for many days afterwards.

Having lots of ideas about turtle soup, we

watched our chance to get a fat snapper. We could never get close enough for a shot with our .22, it seemed, but one day, as we glided under overhanging willows, we saw a turtle sleeping right ahead of us on the bank. As Walt guided the boat closer, I leaned over the bow and, nearly falling out of the canoe, I grabbed it.

Having a third passenger was so much fun we decided to keep it alive until night, so the turtle, whom we named Alice, was jammed up in the curve of the bow, blocked in with our wire cooking grate. Alice kicked and scratched all day, until we shot her. Walt was elected surgeon, to get the brute apart. He started in with the knife, but it was our camp ax that did the work. A can opener probably would have been better. The meat, we found, was all on the upper legs. It was a tough job getting the hide off, but three pounds of meat rewarded us.

We boiled it. Boiling, we learned, is the most practical method of cooking wild animals and fowls when you are in the woods. I had read somewhere that turtle soup should be highly seasoned. So I did that. With the first swallow, Walt let out a howl and jumped for the water bag. Thereafter, we ruled turtle soup off the list of eatables.

Something else I had read about was frying-pan bread. I tried to make it, but I must have mixed things. It was fierce. From then on we used the little flour we had for frying fish. We traded our can of baking powder to a farmer's wife for a loaf of fresh bread, and then and there decided bread would be on the menu permanently.

Three days out, we witnessed a little incident which everyone refuses to believe when I tell it. We saw ahead of us a small animal swimming across the river. We got close enough to see that it was a woodchuck. That was not so strange, for I have seen them swimming before, but one hundred yards further on we saw another little animal swimming in the same direction. We could hardly believe our eyes—it was a baby rabbit! It could not have been more than three or four weeks old. As we slid up beside the poor little fellow, it turned toward the canoe, blindly seeking aid, for it was exhausted. We set it down on the other shore, where it shivered a while, then scampered off into the woods. We decided some animal must have been responsible for these small creatures swimming across. Weeks later, on the Red River, near Canada, we saw a small red squirrel jump into the water and swim against the choppy waves to the opposite shore.

Noon was the best part of the day. We allowed ourselves an hour's rest under the trees, where we always spread out a slicker for a table-cloth and our simple lunch. It was always the same—a loaf of bread, a can of cold beans, and a bit of sweet chocolate.

It was sometimes hard to get up again and out into the hot sun for more paddling against the current, but as Walt put it, "Can you think of any work you would rather do?" We couldn't.

Just before we reached St. Peter, while bucking a stretch of fast water, one of the paddles broke in my hands. It had been cracked from the start. Until we reached Fargo, North Dakota, we had no spare.

As we tied up under the St. Peter bridge, a carload of boys and girls greeted us. We went into a café to buy some bread, and as we waited for it the soothing odor of well-cooked food assailed our nostrils. It proved too much for our outraged appetites. With one agonized look at each other we dived for a table. Sitting back with contented sighs a little later, we decided that every Sunday we would have a real meal, prepared by some one else—provided we were near a town.

Mankato, Minnesota, was reached by noon of the next day, marking the first division point of our trip. It had taken us six days to reach it. And for an eternity of five seconds I was sure Mankato was to be our last point. Then and there our trip almost ended.

Under a highway bridge, the river narrowed to a small channel through which the water poured with a foaming rush. Recklessly we decided to attempt to pole the canoe up through the channel, to first get the force of a back eddy near shore and then to shoot out straight against the current. That was our mistake.

I was in front. I remember shoving out into the main current, but after that things happened almost too fast for my memory to register them. I have a vision, like a fleeting nightmare, of the bow of the canoe lifting miraculously into the air before my nose, shaking and trembling like a harpooned whale and then darting with incredible speed sideways toward the cement bridge support. My memory has retained the picture of the huge cement wall rushing toward me, but how I got my paddle between the wall and the frail boat I cannot explain at all. In a moment we were floating unharmed down stream and I was examining in amazement a chipped paddle and a skinned knuckle.

We were becoming accustomed to being stared at in the towns. Dressed in boots, khaki trousers and shirts, red bandannas around our necks, we must have amazed the inhabitants. We wrote our weekly stories wherever we could, in newspaper offices, garages, stores.

Immediately out of Mankato we passed the Blue Earth River, which flows into the Minnesota, and for a time, at least, the current was less strong. But the sand bars continued, and unless we made all the bends far on the outside, we would ground on the bottom and would have to pole out into the stream again.

We took half a day off at one excellent camping spot and washed the canoe, our clothes and ourselves. Walt had a hard time cleaning his pants because they were of heavy, whipcord material. After I had lost both bars of soap we decided to go swimming.

"Bud! Lookout!" Walt yelled suddenly as we were splashing about merrily. Startled, I glanced toward shore, and there was a herd of cattle making a concentrated rush for us. Somehow, I forgot the water was three feet deep and dived straight for the bottom. When I raised my bruised head the herd was calmly drinking at the shore. Maybe it was just a friendly race to see which one could get the first swallow.

The next night we cooked our first fish—a carp. That is the fish nobody eats. Although this one was a bit gashed, where I hit it with the paddle as it sucked at reeds along the shore, when it was rolled in flour and fried with strips of bacon it was fit for a king.

At New Ulm we met F. W. Johnson, brother of Minnesota's former governor. He told us the history of Riverside Park, where our canoe was docked. The park was the site of the old steamboat landing, when the ships used to come from New Orleans up the Mississippi into the Minnesota. The last steamboat reached New Ulm in 1874. Now the river is much too low.

Leaving New Ulm, we made our first mistake in direction. For two hundred yards we paddled on the old bed of the Minnesota and probably would have gone further had not a group of boys put us right. They were very much amused by our ignorance.

An eighty-two-year-old man, Alec Russell, who lived on a farm twenty miles up river from New Ulm, told us about the Indian uprising of '62, which he had gone through as a young boy. He related how the battle with the enraged red men had swept back and forth between New Ulm and Fort Ridgely, which was further up river. After long fighting, the white men at the village put up anvils and stove pipes, which the Indians believed were cannon. The Sioux were frightened at this display of unexpected power and retreated.

Of course, we had to see the fort, which now is a state park. Only one of the original buildings remains and someone, believing more in being practical than appropriate, had put a tin roof over it. The view of the Minnesota valley was inspiring from the hill on which the fort

24

stood, but we were startled when we saw how much the river ahead twisted and turned.

We reached the village of Morton in darkness in order to buy supplies before the stores closed, as the next day was Sunday. Here no one seemed to be able to tell about the river ahead. One woman thought the river flowed west, but then, she explained, she had only lived there four years. Another woman in a store thought we must be having a wonderfully easy life, doing nothing but sitting in a boat all the time, but when we showed her the ugly sun blisters on our wrists she changed her mind.

On Sunday we ran into a hail and rain storm, our first while traveling. Our poncho kept the outfit dry, and vigorous use of the sponges kept most of the water out of the canoe. We had Sunday dinner in a café again. The waitress sympathized with us so much that she gave us each a piece of pie for nothing.

It was queer that so many people saw only the hardships and discomforts of our trip. No one seemed to realize what great sport it was.

25

## CHAPTER III

## SNAKES!

FOR two days it rained intermittently, and our first portage, a short one of thirty feet over the rocks of the Belleview Falls, was made in a drizzle.

We ran, or dragged the canoe up through eight small rapids that afternoon. In the first one, I was elected to get out and pull, and out I stepped into water up to my hips. I had to change all my clothes at noon in a cold wind. Then we took turns wading. In one stretch, so shallow we could not ride, we pulled the canoe at least a mile. Once, as we paddled close to shore, a small bass jumped clear over the canoe, right in front of my nose.

At night we were dead on our feet and too tired to hunt a good camping spot. We just pulled off our clothes and flopped inside the tent. I was dreaming pleasantly of soft beds and mountains of ice cream, when all of a sudden somebody yelled, "Snakes!" so loudly that I awoke and made a dive for the entrance in the same instant. It was Walt. He was having a nightmare and sat up so suddenly that the whole tent went over. If anyone had been near, he would have certainly been very startled to see two naked young men, shivering and slapping mosquitoes, standing in the moonlight while trying to put up a tent.

We escaped another calamity in the morning. We were almost up through a long rapid. I was in the bow, warding off rocks, when my paddle suddenly pinched between two stones and, to keep from breaking the blade, I let it go.

Lacking forward control, the canoe wheeled about and shot off down stream. I could do nothing but grip the gunwales in futile desperation and trust to Walter and luck. Both were on the job, for while some of the boulders came within inches of the boat, not one of them so much as scraped the side.

We passed the entrance of the Yellow Medicine River and then for twelve miles paddled on still water into Granite Falls, racing the clock in order to beat the closing hour for the grocery

stores. Our camping spot was unique that night
—a grassy bank right in the town's residential
section. Here we wrote another story for the
*Star*.

Leaving town, a group of boys helped us make
a difficult portage over a dam. A number of times
we were helped this way.

By this time we were well accustomed to sitting erect all day long. We had learned to paddle
with easy, rhythmical strokes and our arms did
not ache any more at night. We soon found the
stern seat the more comfortable. My legs were
too long to stretch out in the bow, so when I was
in front I often paddled on my knees. I grew to
like that method, but Walter always preferred
sitting up.

Another jumping fish, a big catfish this time,
would have landed in the canoe (and been eaten
for supper) had it not hit my knee with a resounding smack.

I shall never forget the night of July third.

We pitched tent on a level prairie, several
yards away from the fringe of trees that lined
the river. Noticing that the breeze was rising, we
staked the tent so the entrance faced away from

the wind. Some time after midnight, I was awakened by a flash of lightning. It revealed Walt,
sitting in the entrance, peering out into the
darkness.

"This is going to be some storm," he said. The
wind increased and rain began pattering on the
flapping sides of the tent. Then the storm broke.
Thunder crashed and the rain swept down across
the unprotected field in driving sheets.

Then we heard hoofbeats and remembered a
herd of horses we had noticed grazing when we
retired. Our hearts pounded as the thudding
hoofbeats grew louder and louder. The herd was
bearing down upon us! Could they see the tent
in the blackness? We had no time to think nor
to speak to each other but, quivering, lay flat to
the ground as the sound of the panic-stricken
beasts increased to a roar. And suddenly they
were past, their black forms whistling by on
either side. Their noise died away as quickly as
it had come, and the next flash of lightning
showed our faces, damp with sweat and chalk-
white.

In the wet light of the dawn we found our
canoe, turned completely over and lying half in

the water. Our firewood, covered by a slicker, was soaked and it was necessary to cut more. I remember that well, because I still possess a scar on the back of my left hand where the ax bit into me when it slipped on the wet wood. Had I struck half an inch more toward the center of my hand, I would have severed the cord to my forefinger.

Although we entered our first lake, Lac Qui Parle, that day, which was the Fourth of July, we had no opportunity to see how the *Sans Souci* would behave in waves, for the water was as smooth as glass. It was delightful to paddle on still water for a change. Gliding along the shore, we heard a noise which sounded like a small rapid.

It was, and the sight fascinated us. Hundreds of carp were leaping up and down in the muddy, shallow water of a little lagoon. The place was swarming with them. The temptation was too much. Up went our trouser legs and in we waded with the paddles. We killed five big ones, one weighing about twelve pounds. We saved the best for ourselves and gave the others to a farmer for his chickens, in return for some cold bottles of pop.

Coming out of the lake, the river was very small, running in a channel not more than forty feet wide. There were high weeds on each side and everywhere around us was low, marshy swamp. There was no place to stop. The channel wound crazily, seeming to get nowhere. The reeds prevented a breeze from reaching us and, as there wasn't a sign of a tree, the sun beat down on us unmercifully. Salty perspiration ran down into our eyes and the maddening horse flies bit time and again.

In the middle of the afternoon we came to a bridge and were able to eat our lunch, weak and spent from the ordeal. A group of fishermen questioned us from the bridge top and were so astounded at finding we were going to eat carp that they gave us a pickerel.

We paddled on, raging at the heat and flies, until we came to the little Pomme de Terre, or Potato River, clear as crystal, flowing into the muddy Minnesota. We peeled off our clothes and plunged in. Oh! it felt wonderful on our aching bodies.

We had to hike a mile to a farm for water. An old, sunburned, wrinkled woman, who could barely speak English, told us to get it from a pump in a shed. Only a few loose boards covered the well and around it most of the pigs and chickens on the farm were mulling. But we had no choice, so we filled our water bag. By camp time, the water had become warm and had a sickening taste. We made camp on the only solid piece of ground we could find and pulled lathes from a fence across the river for firewood. We could not sleep because of violent pains produced by the bad water. Morning was hot and although we were parched, we poured out all the water, for fear we might weaken and drink it.

All during the blistering morning we paddled without water. Finally we sighted a farm and I never drank so much at one time in my life. We discovered that the farmer, a young man, had gone to a grade school where my mother had taught, and a few hours later, on another farm, we met a girl who had gone to our high school. Our faces were so burned and blackened that she did not recognize us.

Ten miles away from Ortonville, Big Stone Lake, and the source of the Minnesota River, we camped, anxious to reach the town. It took ten

The *Sans Souci* lodged in the narrowest part of the Minnesota—a half mile from source.

Walt rescues a mired lamb.

(*Right*) Blue heron on Minnesota River.

hours of paddling to do it, for the river was not more than twenty feet wide and it was a hard job to swing our eighteen-foot canoe around the sharp bends. Twice we had to cut our way through fallen branches. Then we made our second mistake in direction when we got on the little Whetstone Creek and dragged the canoe for an hour before Walt realized the error. He was familiar with this country. Ortonville was his home town, although he had left it ten years ago.

At lunch time we saw a little lamb, about an hour old. He was a little black fellow and his legs wobbled under him as he stood beside his mother.

As the light grew weaker toward evening we paddled out into Big Stone Lake and the long fight of three weeks with the Minnesota River was ended. Five hundred miles were behind us and almost one-fourth of the journey was over. From now on we would never have to paddle up stream.

On the South Dakota side of the lake we camped and in the night a terrific storm rolled up the lake. A woman in a near-by cottage told us she had worried about us all night, "sleeping out in that tiny tent." As for us, protected by giant cottonwoods, we slept like logs.

As we made ready to repaint the bottom of the badly scraped canoe, I discovered our paddles were gone. I asked Walt where he had put them.

"Holy Smoke, Bud. Now I remember, I laid them right on the beach and forgot them. The storm must have washed them away."

We were genuinely frightened then, for we had made inquiries and knew there was not a paddle to be bought in the town; but, rowing in a borrowed boat along the shore, we came upon both of them close together, caught in some reeds half a mile away.

We wrote another story for the *Star* which was published under the heading, "Canoeists Victorious in Battle with Minnesota," and said that we were among the few persons who ever had paddled the full length of the river against its current. And, at the editor's request, we wrote a story for the Ortonville paper, also. Oh, we were getting to be real press agents!

We inspected a beautiful lake yacht, remodeled from an old boat that was wrecked in a storm several years ago, when several persons had lost their lives. When Walt was a little kid he used to run away from home for two or three days at a time in order to make the lake trip on that boat. I could hardly drag him away from this one.

As we were about to open a can of beans for our lunch, one of the women in a cottage near by came down to our camp with a hot dinner on a tray. We were so surprised we almost forgot to thank her.

Paddling peacefully up the lake, half dozing in my seat, I was startled from a reverie by a sudden yell from Walt. Right ahead of us, about fifty feet away was what looked like a big black log, slowly sinking from sight. Half asleep though I was I realized that, in general, logs don't have fins and tails that move back and forth. It was a sturgeon, the first either of us had seen. It was at least six feet long.

We were thrilled to the point of momentary paralysis. Then, like excited fools, we began circling and casting our line madly, although we knew a net was the only instrument with which sturgeon could be caught. Even if we had hooked the fish, it probably would have pulled us under water.

Forty miles long and but a mile wide, Big Stone Lake, nestling down among rolling green hills, is beautiful. Lakes in the pine country up north are fascinating, many of them, but theirs is a beauty that is cold and wild. This was peaceful.

Always the Sir Galahad, Walt clambered aboard a motorboat occupied by two girls who apparently could not start their motor. He got it started and the girls, grateful, offered to tow us down the rest of the lake. It was hard to refuse, but we had decided at the start that we were to paddle every inch of the way ourselves.

Now the course of the lake swung northward and a strong wind billowed the white caps behind us. It was our first experience in rough water and it was glorious. Bare from the waist up, with the cool air rushing over us, it was thrilling to shoot along on the big rollers. I thought of all our friends back in the city, studying and working inside, and it was hard to keep from yelling from pure delight.

Darkness found us laboring along in the narrow, weed-choked channel which leads into the village of Brown's Valley. On a heavy, sharp snag, we ran a bad hole in the boat, the only real puncture we suffered all summer. Too tired to cook, we ate in a restaurant where the waitress told us she had read all our stories and was much interested in the trip. We brightened up.

We faced a two-mile portage in the morning, right through the center of town. We loaded each other with pack sacks, realizing we had things very badly arranged for portaging. It looked as if each of us was carrying the furnishings of a four-room flat. At the end of half a mile we were exhausted.

Evidently our expressions registered heavy discouragement for two boys in a big truck stopped and hauled us the rest of the way. There we hid our packs and started back for the canoe. We got a ride back also, with another man who said he would transport the canoe for us, too. That was pretty decent, so we bought him a couple of cigars. We thought he was one of the most pleasant men we had ever met and later we found that he was an "outlaw fisherman."

The waves grew bigger on Lake Traverse, which is twenty miles long, but this time they were against us, which made it hard going. We discovered, much to our joy, that the *Sans Souci* could ride the rollers like cork. We decided then that, if you know the canoe, it is safer in rough water than a heavier boat. Not once all summer did we tip over. We could clamber all over the pile of packs in the canoe without rolling it. We were perfectly at home in the boat.

It was hot that day, and over our coats of tan was added another coat—of bright red sunburn.

Through the reedy channel we pushed our way, into Little Lake Traverse, or, as the neighboring farmers have more appropriately named it, Mud Lake. We camped among a row of deserted hunting cabins and pitched our tent on a nice, grassy front, right beside an artesian well, which provided us with running water. A man approached as we were eating and we thought that perhaps we were to be ejected from the place, but he merely wished to chat. He was another outlaw fisherman, who followed the practice of rowing out at dusk and running long, baited setlines for catfish.

The next day capped our honored list of "toughest days." It was heartbreaking. We simply could not find a channel out of Mud Lake into the Bois de Sioux River. We pushed and poled everywhere through the wall of reeds, higher than our heads, but the water grew more shallow everywhere we tried. Finally, desperate, frenzied from the clouds of mosquitoes in the evil-smelling swamp, we decided there was only one thing to do. We rolled up our trouser legs and, leaving our boots on, we got out and began wading, pushing and pulling the canoe, plunging through the dense reeds, the water and mud up to our hips.

It was a back-breaking experience. At a signal, we heaved with all our strength, perhaps moving the boat six feet. At intervals we stood on muskrat houses and tried to make out the channel, but it was no use. And at other intervals, while one stayed by the canoe the other plunged off on "scouting" expeditions to find the deepest part of the river.

Then we decided we must portage the whole works toward one side of the swamp or the other. We decided to go east. First we rested for a long time. Then we loaded with the heavier packs. Before starting out we tied a rag on the tallest reed we could find, so we would not lose the canoe. Then we set out. At each step, the weight of the packs forced us deep into the muck. Each step was a desperate effort. Should we fall, the packs would sink deep in the soft mud and we would never get them upon our backs again. When I felt that I could not stand another moment, we broke through into a clearing, and there, at our feet, coursed a clear stream of water.

We almost wept with relief.

## CHAPTER IV

# *TRAGEDY—ALMOST*

AFTER many minutes, when we felt strength returning to our bodies, we began to wade back to the canoe, first tying another rag to a high reed. Forcing the canoe to the channel was more difficult yet, although we could rest at any time. Each took an end and then with a "Heave Ho!" we lifted and plunged forward a few steps. About thirty plunges and we were there. Dropping exhausted to a bit of solid ground, we did not get up for half an hour.

Provided with dry trousers and wool socks (many pairs of the latter are necessary on a canoe trip) we poled and pushed and dodged rocks along the narrow, twisting, shallow stream for an hour until we found ourselves up against another solid wall of tall reeds and more wading ensued.

The Bois de Sioux was swarming with ducks,

big ones and broods of youngsters, and it was laughable to watch their system of escaping us. At a signal from the mother, all the little fellows scattered and dived, coming up as far away as possible, and in the reeds along the narrow channel if they could reach them. Meanwhile the mother would be swimming madly back and forth before the canoe, pretending she was unable to fly, and all the while leading us farther from her family. But once we followed a little duckling, and as he rose to the surface Walt grabbed him. He wasn't a bit frightened; he kicked and pecked at Walt and stared him balefully in the eye. When loosed, he did not rush away but calmly swam off with great dignity.

Before nightfall, which arrived on the wings of millions of mosquitoes, we had lost the channel and found it again several times. We learned to not always follow the stretches of open water but to try to find which way the current was seeping. We would brush aside the thick green scum on the surface and endeavor to see which way the particles along the bottom were drifting. We were able to reach a pasture and camp on the edge of the swamp. Most of the chilly night was

spent in hunting down mosquitoes with the flash-
light and murdering them.

Although it was mid-July, the morning
dawned cold and raw and a strong north wind
blew against us. The day before we had made
seven miles in as many hours and this day we
made about eleven until afternoon, simply repeat-
ing the process of the previous day.

After Fairmount, North Dakota, where we
replenished our grub supply, we had a real channel to follow, although it was half filled with
reeds and had no current. It was hard to believe
that we were going downhill, but it was true, as
we had crossed the big divide at Big Stone Lake.
On the other side, the rivers flow east and south,
on this the only big river flows straight north, the
Red River of the North, and the real source of it
is the Bois de Sioux. The only rivers in the world
that flow directly north are said to be the Nile in
Egypt and the Red River of the North, besides a
few smaller streams.

We tried a modernized form of tracking a
canoe. We tied the middle of a small, strong,
seventy-foot rope to the prow of the canoe and
each took an end. Walt walked in Minnesota

and I in North Dakota, towing the boat at a faster rate than we could paddle it.

When the river grew wider and acquired a slight current, we climbed in. At every bend, however, it was very shallow, so that we had to wade, lifting and pushing the canoe. It was extremely tiring work, but at night, with our stomachs full of boiled snapping turtle and hot tea, things looked cheerful.

At Wahpeton, North Dakota, the Bois de Sioux and the Otter Tail rivers join. This junction forms what is called the beginning of the Red River. We repaired a broken brace, then pushed off eagerly into the speeding current.

The willows whirled by us as we dug our paddles savagely, thrilled at the ease with which the miles passed. Seven hundred miles of this lay ahead. Who said this trip was hard?

Crun-n-nch! With a suddenness that threw us forward in our seats, we rammed high up on a gravel bed. So—there was a catch in it? There certainly was, for we found the river full of similar gravel bars which necessitated careful watching of the route ahead or we would tear the *Sans Souci* full of holes.

Late in the afternoon we checked our rushing speed to lift out a blue jay, fluttering helplessly in the water at the edge of the steeply banked shore. It was too tired to rise from the water alone.

Camp was made above a fast, shallow stretch, the first "rapid" we would run down through. In the morning, after carefully studying it, we negotiated it successfully and felt like veterans. If we had only known then what lay ahead!

We thoroughly enjoyed that day of paddling with a strong current, along banks that oozed with the "Red River mud" which we had heard so much about. Hundreds of frogs covered the banks and finally the idea of frog legs for supper popped into our heads. Frogs have more lives than a cat and some of them I must have cracked over the head a dozen times before killing them.

Several little farm boys waded across the river to our camp with a gift of half a dozen eggs and a pail of fresh milk. And so, when the dishes were washed, we all sat around the fire while Walt played "Golden Slippers," and all the other songs the boys could suggest, on his mouth organ.

Their eyes shone as we told them of some of our experiences, which made us feel like a couple of big chiefs.

To see how much the river actually did bend around, we set the compass before us and watched it. We were supposed to be traveling north, but we went west, east and sometimes straight south. About the only northward distance we gained was on the turns. We paddled over thirty miles one day, covering but ten miles by road.

The current grew sluggish and remained so the entire length of the river. In the heavy soft mud of the shore we continually observed carcasses of pigs, cows and sometimes dogs, that had become mired and died there. At times the stench was dreadful. Herds of cattle would wade into mid-stream, seeking relief from the flies. We would drive the canoe toward them with all our speed, and just before we reached them they would dash for shore, with an uproar of splashing and snorting. It was great sport.

But once the cows fooled us. They didn't get out of the way and as we were going too fast to stop quickly we rammed right into their midst. You can imagine. For a few seconds I could see

46

nothing but a tossing storm of horns and hoofs. A rain of spray struck us, backed by resounding blows from switching tails. Hoofs thudded along the side of the canoe. When the storm was over and we had removed the mud and water from our faces, we saw that the boat had not been damaged.

July seventeenth—one month on the trail and seven hundred miles gone by.

We were five miles from Fargo, North Dakota, the largest city we would visit, with the exception of Winnipeg, Manitoba. We prepared for the city by bathing in the cool, clean stream which now had taken on new character because it was backed up from a dam at Fargo.

In a downpour of rain we entered Fargo. Our first act was the purchasing of another paddle, a five-foot blade, wide and heavy. As protection against possible splintering, we had it reinforced with a strip of heavy copper over the end. Now each of us had an excellent, durable paddle.

An encouraging letter from the *Star* awaited us. That night, we stayed at the home of relatives, and slept between sheets. It was so soothing we refused to awake until noon. And the food! I am afraid the grocery bills took a decided leap while Walt and I were there. Everyone seemed astounded at our appetites. For breakfast we consumed—each of us—twenty pancakes! It was an unforgivable thing to do, considering the fact that we were guests, but anything less would have been an insult to our stomachs.

Before starting out again we had our first haircuts in a month. We had it done in a barber college in order to save money. Moral: don't have your hair cut in barber colleges. But even if we did look like Tom Sawyer after Aunt Polly's bowl-over-the-head treatment, it didn't bother us much.

We said good-by to all of our kind hosts. The boat was loaded down with cookies, fruit and jam, even cake—everything a canoeist is not supposed to eat.

Next morning we were back in town, after a sad experience. Several days before, a fly had bitten Walt on the lower part of his right thumb. Constant rubbing against the paddle had irritated the sore and that night, six miles north of Fargo, Walt decided he must do something for it, as the pain was increasing. Long nights of drug-store work, necessary to keep him in school, had acquainted him with many emergency-relief measures and as we turned in that night he applied a poultice of soap and sugar, tied over his hand.

I awoke at midnight with a sense of having heard strange noises and as I listened I realized they were coming from Walt, curled up beside me. At first I thought he was mumbling in his sleep and prepared to settle down again. Then I knew he was moaning. I realized then that he must be suffering awfully and felt ashamed for having made light of his injury. I sat up most of the night, trying to think what to do next, for it must be serious. Nothing less could make Walt flinch.

In the morning we removed the poultice. It had accomplished nothing and now his thumb, brown and discolored, had swollen so it resembled the thumb on a boxing glove. Back to Fargo we had to go. We hid the outfit in the bushes and dragged the canoe well up on the bank, threw our sweaters over our shoulders, and started the hike to town. After a month of sitting, the walking was miserable enough for me, but the constant jar on his infected hand, which he held with the other, must have been agony for poor Walt.

It was Sunday, but an inquiry in the first drug store produced the address of a doctor who was in his office. While Walt was in the physician's waiting room, I went out and phoned my relatives to tell them of our return. When I came back, I found Walt and the doctor, a tall, stout, jovial person, talking as if they were old friends. By that time, of course, the doctor knew all about our trip.

"Meet Doctor Gronvold," Walt said, as he sat in the operating chair. "This is my partner, Arnold Sevareid, doctor."

"Sevareid?" he questioned. "For Heaven's sake, boy, I know your dad."

And he did. It happened that he had been raised on a farm next to my grandfather's, in southeastern Minnesota.

"Well, well," he said, laughing, "I'm certainly glad you came to me. And it's a lucky thing, too, for another day without attention and this boy would be in the hospital."

Well, we spent exactly eleven days more in Fargo, most of the time as the guests of Doctor Frederick Gronvold. What a host he was! Every day he treated Walt's hand and every afternoon drove us out to our camp to see if our outfit was all right.

At night, when Walt and I entered the office, we would find candy, soft drinks and magazines awaiting us, with usually a couple of theater tickets stuck in the midst of the other gifts. Later, the doctor would come in and the three of us would sit for hours, sometimes until nearly morning, talking about the woods, hunting and fishing, dogs, horses, canoes, anything at all connected with outdoor life, a subject on which the doctor was an authority.

The more I think of it, the more I wonder at his generosity and kindness of heart, for he had never seen us before. Of course it was useless to try to pay him for his services.

I remember one night we found a note lying on our davenport in his office. It read: "Dear boys, sleep as late in the morning as you want to. If the office girl disturbs you, tell her to jump in the lake."

When, at the end of eleven days, Walt's hand was almost healed, and we decided we must be off, the parting with the doctor was hard. I am sure there were tears in his eyes, and I know there were tears in mine, and in Walt's. Half a mile away, at the first bend, we turned and saw his tall figure at the water's edge. He was still watching us.

The doctor's parting words repeated themselves in my brain continually during the rest of the day: "Don't let anyone, no matter who he is, convince you that your trip can't be completed. You have youth and strength, and courage too, I hope, and with a little common sense you can do it."

Handling the paddle gingerly with his injured hand, Walt was able to help thrust the canoe along, but we had to go slowly. We were two weeks behind our schedule. The first of August was at hand and as we progressed northward, the nights began to be chilly.

## CHAPTER V

## RED RIVER MUD

THE journey down the Red River from Fargo had been almost uneventful, a long, monotonous process of steady paddling, with no current to aid us, around unending bends, under a hot sun, beside muddy banks. Our only relaxations from duty were a meeting with an old school pal on a farm north of Fargo, where we stopped a few hours, and a day's visit at the town of Crookston, at the home of more relatives of mine.

By a lucky coincidence, it happened that my father put in a long-distance telephone call to Crookston, an hour after we had arrived there. How queer it was to talk with my parents, back in Minneapolis! After weeks of paddling, it had seemed that we were thousands of miles away from home, and out of touch with everyone there. Now I felt that we hadn't gone so far after all.

After a moment Dad said, "If you feel like giving it up, Bud, we'll understand."

"Give it up! Why, the best part of the trip is ahead of us, Dad! Honestly, we like it. And we're going to go all the way to the bay, too."

"Attaboy," Walt whispered, at my elbow.

"All right, go ahead, but please don't take too many chances. Promise us."

Stop at the halfway mark, with a great big slice of northern Canada waiting to be explored? Not us!

The sentiment in Minneapolis now was that we would never reach Hudson Bay, because it was getting so late in the year. I remember receiving a letter from a boy at a resort, where I had worked the year before. It read, "The boss wants to bet you won't get there. Shall I take him up on it?" The answer was, of course, in the affirmative.

Leaving Crookston and Grand Forks, we ran into a very trying time for our nerves and tempers—the fly time. Black house flies infested everything for a week. All day, as we swung our paddles in the sun, they swarmed about our faces and half-bared bodies; and as soon as we had made preparations for a meal they called a convention and congregated on all the food in sight.

Walt's hand was now practically healed. With a letter of introduction from Dr. Gronvold, we visited the offices of another physician in Crookston, where the thumb was again dressed. We had a suspicion the letter did more than just introduce us, for this doctor also refused payment. Even though we were miles away, Dr. Gronvold was still intent on helping us. We thought about our steadily weakening finances, and we let the Crookston doctor have his own way.

North of the town of Grand Forks, we coasted by an Indian woman washing clothes in the river, surrounded by her children. We met Indians later on, in primitive conditions, but these in the midst of civilization were the handsomest of all. Tall and straight, with long black hair and fine facial features, they were the characters of *Hiawatha* come to life.

The district into which we now made our way was inhabited almost entirely by Polish farmers. They lived in scanty, peasant fashion. All had deep wells, from which they drew their water by hand in long pails attached to the end of ropes. One family we remember well—at least I do. I was sitting back in the boat, with my legs sprawled over the gunwales, wearing nothing but a pair of dirty trousers. The canoe was beached while Walt was taking his turn at getting water at a farm. I thought, a few minutes later, that I heard him shout something about "shirts" but I paid no attention. The next moment I heard shrieks of laughter—feminine laughter. I dived for my clothes. There, at the summit of the bank, were five young Polish ladies, with Walt very much at home amidst them, wearing a large grin as he saw my blushing countenance.

Ordinarily we traveled on the river bare from the waist up, except for red bandanna kerchiefs, soaked with cool water, knotted about our necks. We had noticed with growing interest that whenever we came in sight of a group of children playing or fishing on the banks, they immediately turned and ran up into the woods. We realized they were frightened, but could not understand why.

One little fellow explained it. He came trembling out of the bushes, after we had called for a long time. "Gee!" he said, through quivering lips, "we thought you wuz Injuns."

Near Drayton, North Dakota, we passed through a pontoon bridge, the only one we came across all summer. A dozen large scows with boarded tops were linked together, leaving a small aperture between each sloping end, through one of which we slipped, heads lowered.

At Drayton Walt received some news, thrilling, but very, very disconcerting. We sat at a table in a little café, and he read me the letter. It was from a teacher in our high school.

"We have succeeded in getting a two-year scholarship to the University of Chicago for you, worth approximately fifteen hundred dollars. Since you are making your own struggle for an education, we know how much this will mean to you. You must be in Chicago by the last week in September to take advantage of it."

My ejaculations of joy choked in my throat as I heard the closing sentence. The last week in September! It was then August 8.

Walt said nothing, but kept his eyes upon the paper. I did not know what to say, either. But I could feel what was going on in his mind— knew that the outcome of our trip depended upon his next words. It was not my place to urge any course of action. I would not protest any decision he made.

He was still silent. I wandered to the window, mechanically paid the clerk and stared at the front page of a newspaper without knowing what I was reading. It seemed an eternity before I heard the scraping of his chair. We walked together down to the river without speaking to each other. But as we slid our paddles from under a bush, he said: "No. We'll have to try to finish. If we don't get back in time, we just don't, that's all. But we can't quit now."

After that, we hardly spoke of the matter again.

We went on. Fifteen miles ahead, we rounded a curve and behold! On the bank were dozens of children and older people, grouped around mountains of cake, pickles and ice-cream freezers. It was a Sunday-school picnic.

"Here come those guys from Missouri!" one little boy shouted.

We didn't bother to explain, since they were kind enough to invite us to their feast. As a reward, we gave all our hosts a canoe ride.

That night was cold and it brought with it a chill of worry into our hearts. Already it was late in the year. We were less than halfway to our goal. We vowed that no more picnics or other diversions, however tempting, would cut down our traveling time, but that every available minute would be spent in hard paddling.

We were near the Canadian border and a single day's travel would put us on foreign soil. But again we were forced to take time out, this time, however, in a good cause.

We had seen many carcasses of mired livestock and now we came across live sheep, their slim legs held fast, deep in the leadlike mud of the river banks. Within one day we pulled out four animals. It was muddy, disagreeable work and the sheep did not seem to like it any more than we did, but it meant saving their lives and we would have been heartless had we gone on without trying to rescue them. Once we even rescued a cow!

At the next town we recommended to the newspaper editor that he print a warning to farmers that they patrol the river banks regularly, or provide adequate fencing, because the number of

dead animals along the shore was appalling. He
promised to do so.

That day it was nice and cool in the shade at
lunch time—so nice that Walt fell asleep. Finally, I stirred myself enough to pick up the
utensils and make for the river. There was the
*Sans Souci,* floating peacefully down stream, a
hundred yards away. I removed my clothes and
swam for it. I did not bother to dress when we
began paddling again.

Three bends farther on we came upon a large
Jersey cow lying in an awkward heap at the
water's edge, raising her head at intervals to take
a gasping breath, then letting it fall back under
water.

The animal was mired almost to the hips and
its neck muscles were weakening. Clearly, it
would soon drown.

Being dressed only in a pair of white trunks, I
was naturally elected to wade into the oozing
mud and try to hold the struggling animal's head
out of water while Walt went to search for a farmer and a rope. It was a tough job. The cow's
heaves nearly upset me and the clouds of horse
flies swarming about the Jersey turned their attention to my bare skin.

After what seemed ages, Walt appeared with a man, a rope and a halter.

To our surprise the man immediately sat down and laughed, "Yah, that's old lame Nancy. She sure got herself in a fix this time, didn't she?" He was an imbecile. Then he said, "Maybe we better shove her off in the current, huh? She ain't no good to us, anyhow."

But I wasn't going to let the cow drown, valuable or not, after all my effort. Walt couldn't see the farmer's point, either, so with a nod to me, he slipped on the halter, and the two of us hauled her clear of the water. Ignoring the farmer, we went in search of higher authority and were rewarded by two large dishes of ice cream.

In the morning we were in Pembina, North Dakota, one of the historic villages of the state. Here it was that a group of Scotchmen, coming down from Hudson Bay in search of fur had settled. Advised that films would cost a few cents more across the line, we stocked up all we would need.

Two miles on, we bribed a little child to take a snapshot of us "in the act of crossing into Canada."

It was the twelfth day of August, when Walt

and I checked our outfit through the customs office at Emerson, Manitoba, and entered Canada. Since our start, June seventeenth, we had covered approximately one thousand miles.

Upon our formal entry, customs officials declared us to be the first ever to enter from the United States by canoe since that customs office had been established. Our appearance and meager outfit puzzled them, but we escaped trouble because we had secured a letter of introduction and explanation from the Canadian agent in Minneapolis.

We did not, however, get through without paying a deposit of five dollars and a quarter on our canoe, "which would be returned if we came back with the canoe." Our little .22 caliber rifle they allowed us to take in, for which we were grateful. The canoe deposit represented one-fourth of the boat's value. We named as low a figure as we dared.

As we walked, with our paddles, past a tourist's car with a Minneapolis license plate, it amused us very much to hear one of the small occupants exclaim in a guarded whisper to his mother, "Gee, look at the Canadians. Maybe they're trappers or somep'n."

The inspector who came down to the river hardly bothered to look through our outfit, so engrossed was he with the story of our trip. We took him, upon his request, for a short ride, at the end of which he was forced to go ashore upon the shoulders of Walt, because of the mud.

By camp time we had penetrated seven miles into the new country. We asked a girl sitting on the porch of a little farmhouse for water, and when she said, "in the stable," we knew the people were French. I remembered that in my French textbook at school, the barn, was always "stable." So to the boy of our own age there, I immediately tried out my "parley-voo."

"*Nous sommes Americains,*" I said, which seemed about the easiest.

"Oh, I see," he answered, in perfect English, as Walt kicked me in the shins.

## CHAPTER VI

## *READY FOR THE PLUNGE*

ON my first morning in Canada I received a great thrill—I saw my first wild deer. A little jumper, it was drinking from the river when we came upon it. After the first little yelp of surprise, we remained breathlessly quiet while Walt silently unleashed the camera and I eased the canoe along the willow brush for a close-up. He leaped up the hill, but there, luckily, stopped, staring at us curiously with great brown eyes, while Walt snapped the camera. It struck us as the first sign from nature that we were nearing the northland.

Now we were approaching the city of Winnipeg, one of the high spots of our itinerary and, as we paddled, we talked of what we would do there. We would not waste time in recreation, at movies, or anything like that. Some discouragement about going on, from officials at Emerson, had made us all the more determined to make the bay before the freeze-up.

So, from the border to the city, we traveled ten hours a day, with few rests or stops, through one of the most delightful stretches we had encountered all summer. The water, almost motionless, was clear and cold, the river was wide, and the banks were heavy with green foliage.

Most interesting of all were the little French villages and the French people we met on the farms and in the hamlets. They were a picturesque lot, living and dressing much as I had imagined the inhabitants of France do, and their musical language fascinated us. One old man, short, dark, and bewhiskered, operated a clumsy old ferry at St. Jean (all the villages are named after saints) and he might have stepped out of the pages of Victor Hugo.

We were excited, that night, when we camped fifteen miles from the city. We wanted to see big buildings, lots of people and bright lights again, and we were curious to see how the people of the city would take our idea of paddling to Hudson Bay. And then, Winnipeg represented our first real "jumping-off" place, and we would have to leave prepared for many weeks. At the small posts north of the city, we knew, food and other needy articles were sold only at very high prices.

As we slid into the bank that night, we noticed a long deep dent in the mud where another craft had stopped. After a minute's examination we knew it was a canoe's, and we determined to catch the owners before we reached the city if possible. Since they were canoeing, they would know where we could find the sportsmen of the city and just what kind of a welcome we could expect.

That night we heard one of the most thrilling things either of us ever had listened to—the call of the whippoorwill. It was the first time for each of us and the solitary note, unrepeated, made us sit bolt upright in the tent and stare at each other.

Within ten miles we caught the travelers who had left their sign behind them. Two clean-looking, athletic boys, they gave us full directions for locating ourselves in the city. With their names as references, we were to stop at the Canoe Club.

66

Within the city limits, coasting along through parklike surroundings, a man yelled from a diving float, "Where you bound for?" And when we had shouted the answer, he came back with, "You're crazy! It will be frozen up before you get there."

At the beautiful, spacious Canoe Club, we were taken right into the "family" of more than a thousand members. Sam Southern, the "skipper," we found to be very hospitable. Caretaker, canoe builder and repairer, as well as unofficial father of all troubles and fount of all wisdom about the place, he immediately took charge of us, fixed up our boat on a suitable rack and granted permission for us to camp beside the club. In another tent, alongside ours, was "Tim" Buffington, the Winnipeg movie censor, who seemed to take an interest in us and drove us to the downtown district on more than one occasion.

Sam showed us all the different types of canoes and paddles, which made our equipment look sick, although we refused to admit it. There were war canoes, which contain fourteen men, Peterboroughs, Sunnysides, Old Townes, like ours, and Chestnut freighters. One little canoe was only twelve feet long, a one-man trapper or prospector boat and had to be paddled from the middle.

We liked the city very much, in our two days there. The evenings we spent lolling near the club dock, watching the young men and women swim and paddle or play golf and tennis or dance, were unforgettable since everyone treated us like guests. But they were dangerous. Until now we had thought of only the great adventure we were on, but now we grew a trifle homesick for these soft pleasures of city life. Had we stayed there much longer, probably we might have given up, for protestations were hammered upon us by men there who urged us to quit the trip, "for our own sakes."

Outstanding in our memories of the city is the visit to the mayor's office. We had a letter from the mayor of Minneapolis and we presented it with due gravity—or with as much as we knew how to muster. The mayor's secretary said, "What's this, another freak American endurance stunt?" When he saw the surprised expressions on our faces and learned details of the trip, he apologized laughingly.

Before the start, we had considered making our trip something of a "good-will tour," which somebody always seems to be making, and presenting letters from Minneapolis officials to authorities in each town. But that seemed to cheapen the adventure of it and take away the pure sport, so we discarded the plan.

In a search for maps of Lake Winnipeg and the district north of it, we visited the Manitoba Bureau of Mines in the beautiful Parliament building. We could find no photographic maps, but decided that we could get them at Beren's River or at the lake's end, Norway House. The woman clerk was horrified when she learned our complete plans for paddling to the bay and did not hesitate to express her feeling.

"Why, two boys like you can never reach the bay," she declared. "I know a group of men, a government party, who knew the country, that was lost for a week in Playgreen Lake, and you have to go through that before you get to Norway House. Every year trappers and prospectors, experienced men, get lost in that north country. Why don't you just paddle up to Beren's River, visit around there for a little

69

while and then come back? It's a charming place."

Up to now I had tried to hold out bravely. But this was about the last straw. Not that the woman's reasons were so frightening, but it seemed that no one, anywhere, would encourage us. And when I saw Walt's face droop into a discouraged gloom, my heart sank.

Our savior from mental defeat came in the person of a little, shriveled prospector whom we met the next day in the land office of the post-office building, where we were searching for more maps and information. He was Herb Cowan, sandy-haired, freckled, and he was registering claims. He had come from his permanent camp, east of the Hayes River, close to the bay and along the streams we would have to traverse.

"Why sure, boys, you can make it. Only you can't go through the Hayes on those maps you got there. And be careful as the devil on Lake Winnipeg. You'll sail along on a calm day and woof!—a squall will blow up in ten minutes."

When we told him that everyone said we would be frozen in, he said, "Well, I dunno how fast you can travel, but you look like you can do

as much a day as I can.  Providin' you don't get
lost up there—it's a bad mess of lakes and rivers
—you should make it all right."

With promises to meet him at Norway House,
we fairly ran out of the place in our eagerness to
hit the trail.  In a few minutes, rushing from
store to store, we ordered our full month's supply of grub, more ammunition for the rifle, and
other things, and headed back to the Canoe Club.

It was five in the afternoon when we said
good-by and shoved off.  Probably we should
have waited for morning, but time was precious
to us now and every hour meant much. As we
dipped our paddles after shaking everybody's
hand, we heard a cheer and turned to see a score
of the club members in a huddle, giving us their
send-off yell.

Squalls, rapids or freeze-up—we were on our
way!

That night we camped not far from the city
limits, eager for morning and the further adventures that awaited us.  For now we *were* getting
into the land of adventures.

When we passed through Selkirk the next
day, a Sunday, we said good-by to the last real

town we would see for weeks. We also passed Fort Gary, where, many years before, explorers and traders came and settled after threading their way from Hudson Bay, along exactly the route we were to follow. We stopped to chat with a man in a Peterborough. He was another prospector, a friend of Herb Cowan, and he also assured us that we could get through if we traveled hard and used our heads and compass.

For the first and probably the last time in our lives, we went through the lock of a dam. The St. Andrews dam, near Selkirk, is a long, high cement wall with one lock, at an end, about ninety feet in length. We had been instructed at the club to insist upon being put through, as any craft sixteen feet long or more has that privilege. The gates were opened for us and in we paddled, to sink slowly down alongside the cement wall, grasping a rope to insure against an upset. When we were on the level of the river below the dam, the huge gates swung slowly open and we paddled solemnly out. It must have looked ridiculous—all those tons of water pouring in and out just for our little shell.

Then for miles we floated through low, swampy country, with hardly a decent camping place ever in view. For a time, before the wind slowed them down, we traveled along with a young married couple on a trip to Winnipeg Beach. The man showed us a new steering stroke used by everyone in that district. At the end of the pull, the stern man flicks his blade to the outside, and after practicing for many hours I learned to make the twist, forced by the wrist alone. Walt, however, preferred the method we had been using, an inside flick of the blade.

At dark we camped, very tired, in a small cleared place in the swamp, next to a deserted hut. We were on the forks of the Red River, the point where three main channels carry the stream into the lake. Mosquitoes were bad, but it was to be the last time they ever bothered us all summer.

The Red River of the North, before it finally empties into Lake Winnipeg, disintegrates into innumerable small channels, which flow in all directions through the lowlands. For this reason, members of the club had been careful to hunt up, for us, a large scale map of the district, drawn on canvas.

So, as we sat before our camp fire we carefully studied the drawing and decided on our course for the morning. We determined to follow the steamboat channel, if we could tell it from the others, until we sighted the first of two lighthouses. We had been impressed with the stories told us at the club of duck hunters who had been lost for days in the mess of streams.

We had no trouble. That made us realize more than ever something we had been coming to believe since our start—that residents of each region are prone to exaggerate the dangers of their particular piece of the river or country. At first we were duly impressed, but after leaving Winnipeg we determined to combine, with the advice of others, our own judgment and experience in weighing the benefits and dangers of different routes.

Two small, white lighthouses, one a quarter of a mile directly inland from the other, mark the entrance to the lake. The lighthouse nearer the lake is smaller, so at night a ship coming in from the lake lines up the flickering light of the first with the tower light of the second, and with them as a guide, comes safely up the narrow channel into the river.

The feeling of immensity that overwhelmed me when I first gazed out on Lake Winnipeg, returns to me every time I think of the moment when Walt and I paddled around a bend and for the first time saw the huge body of water we were about to traverse in a frail canoe.

It may as well have been the Atlantic Ocean. My feeling was one of immediate emptiness in the pit of the stomach, and I have a sneaking hunch Walt's impression was not much more optimistic. As far around as we could see stretched water and nothing but water—more water than either of us had ever seen at one time before. But it couldn't be more than three or four hundred miles up to the other end around the east shore line and miles were miles, on river or lake.

A warning about the lake that had come to us even before we left Minneapolis returned to me. It was from a nationally known authority on canoe travel to whom I had written for advice. He answered my letter, saying it would be foolhardy to attempt to navigate the shores of Lake

Winnipeg in a canoe because we would be laid up for weeks at a time in bad weather.

With the ready permission of the lighthouse keeper, who smiled grimly at our plan of navigating the lake in our little craft, we took several pictures from the top of the lighthouse. From the summit we could see more water than ever. The keeper, a crippled Canadian war veteran, scoffed at our ideas and then finally compromised with, "Well, you *might* make it. But none of them Canoe Club fellows ever done it, far as I know."

He had spent years beside the lake and it was his God. He seemed to resent the idea of anything smaller than a hundred-foot steamer audaciously attempting to sail out upon its broad surface. As we were about to embark, he said, scrutinizing the dull skies, "Well, boys, I dunno, I don't like the looks of that mackerel sky. Maybe you better hold over a day or so."

We thanked him, but shoved out. We didn't tell him that men in Winnipeg had warned us of his lonely life, and consequently his love of company at any expense.

With the keeper's warnings ebbing slowly out

of our minds, we navigated straight out a quarter of a mile until we were around a long cribbing. Then, at an angle to the shore, we headed out into the vastness of Lake Winnipeg.

## CHAPTER VII

# INTO THE LAND OF THE CREE

ONE warning we did not forget was that about sand bars. The south end of the lake, out as far as a mile from shore, is infested with bars and in any kind of rough weather, once you let your canoe slide upon them, you are bound to be swamped. Oh, there was a difference in lake paddling! And there was a science to it. We learned fast—we had to.

On our second jump, to Balsam Bay, the waves began coming in from the side and as minutes went by they gained in size. Taken at the wrong moment, we were apt to receive the white crest of the breaker right over our packs and our legs. Our paddling had to be carefully timed and we had to sit lightly in the boat, relaxed at the hips, and allow it to roll all it pleased. That is the secret of successful rough-water canoeing. If you try to decide for your craft how to roll

78

with the waves, soon you find a large portion of the lake in the boat. Let alone, a canoe that is wide enough rides the waves like a cork.

However, when a canoe is loaded down as heavily as the *Sans Souci* was when we entered the lake, a little clever manipulation in the waves is occasionally necessary also. If we saw a breaker was going to hit us at the wrong moment, we rolled the canoe with our hips away from the wave. Though at times our angle was precarious, we saved ourselves many wettings.

Our first pine country! How it thrilled me, when, as we neared Balsam Bay, I could make out the tall, straight spires of green stretching for miles along the rocky, uneven shore line, fading away in a haze to the north! Born and raised on the prairies, never before had I actually been among the pines, and the sight of them sent my blood racing.

Who could have turned back in country like this? It was beautiful. The water was cold; tiny, rocky islands of granite, with a few scraggly birch and spruce topping them, dotted the lake as far as we could see. The waves sloshed up on the rocks with a steady, resounding rhythm; overhead hawks circled and dived, and occasionally, when we came in close, we could hear animal noises within the dark forest.

Winnipeg—"muddy water"—the Crees called it. But we loved it.

Ahead of us we could see among the bobbing breakers a canoe with two men. Bucking the waves directly now, we caught them. We had seen them before at the club. They were on their way to Victoria Beach to spend a brief vacation, and the rest of the day we paddled along with them. They used double-bladed paddles and we tried them for a short while, but gave up in disgust. On a smooth lake, I suppose they are all right, but in rough weather they are unwieldy and in a rapid, of course, they would mean suicide.

After nearly eleven hours of paddling we stopped, at dark, and beached the *Sans Souci* in a little, wind-sheltered cove near Victoria Beach, forty miles up the lake. It was grand, preparing supper on the hard sand of the beach, with the dark forest wall a few yards away at our backs. No grass nor underbrush to clear away, no bugs dropping from the trees, and because of the openness and cool breeze no mosquitoes to disturb our slumber.

Birch bark had always been a magic substance to me, known only from the pages of northern books. Now it was a reality, and I seized the opportunity to start my first camp fire with the bark. It was a proud moment.

"How are we going to put up the tent in this sand?" Walt asked with a puzzled look.

"We don't need any tent," I replied, the realization coming only an instant before the words. Why should we? No mosquitoes, and if it rained we could draw our heads under the rubber poncho which covered our blankets.

Beside us, as we lay on the sand between our blankets and looked straight up at the cold stars, were our gun and ax. For exactly what use they would be employed we were not quite sure, but we had vague imaginings, acquired from books and stories, of prowling bears or wolves which might pilfer from our grub box, even though they did no harm to us. Knowing that from now on until the end of the trip we would be near all kinds of wild animals, we began right by lodging our grub box in a small tree.

81

After the novelty of sleeping without covering wore off, I dropped off to slumber, visions of moose and wildcats stampeding the camp flitting across my tired mind.

"Grab the gun!" Walt was whispering in my ear some hours later.

"There's something thrashing around in that clump of brush," he confided while I stared breathlessly, nearly bending the rifle in my desperate grip. My gaze was frozen on the bushes.

Then, with a rush, a black object tore out of the trees and skittered across the beach, about a yard from our hastily withdrawn heads.

It was a skunk!

The resort at Victoria Beach was the last white-inhabited place we would see for nearly another two hundred miles, and we said so on postcards we sent home. It must have cheered the folks!

After wading and dragging the boat across the shallow channel that separates Elk Island from Victoria Beach, we faced a problem. There was Traverse Bay ahead of us. Either we could paddle around it, sticking close to shore, a trip which would take us the rest of the day, or we could make the six-mile jump to Devil's Island, faintly visible across the water.

We found that it was the custom of canoeists who proposed making the dangerous jump to ask advice of an Indian at a small fishing shack on the point. But the Indian could not be located, so we made the jump anyway. We knew that we must take chances if we hoped to reach Hudson Bay and this seemed as good a place to begin as anywhere. We paddled with all our strength and reached the island winded, although a growing breeze from the south made it difficult and dangerous going the last mile.

As darkness began to settle down over the water and forest, we steered our way through the innumerable rock reefs that stretch out from the shore to a camp spot on the beach, four miles from the Sandy River Indian settlement. The beach was pockmarked everywhere with the tracks of moose and deer, in fact there was no place one could stand and be more than ten feet away from a line of tracks.

We were dozing off with our noses under the poncho when Indians, having seen our dying

camp fire, called to us from out on the water.
We couldn't understand them at first until finally
one who could speak some English made it
known that they were searching for a fishing
boat. Listening to the boat's description we recalled seeing it in the distance at noon, heading
north. We could not make them understand we
were heading for Hudson Bay, as they had never
heard of it, so we simply yelled, "Norway
House." Even that surprised them, for few Indians from the south end of the lake ever had
visited Norway House.

The next morning Walt and I came as close
to death as I ever wish to be. Stripped to the
waist, heavy boots on our feet, we were following
the shore line which ran due north. Walt was in
the bow. A steadily increasing wind from the
south kicked up the waves higher and higher.
The logical thing to do would have been to stick
close to shore, but it was impossible, as reefs ran
out a mile into the surging lake. Once around
them, visible only when we could distinguish between the white spray they caused and the white
of the breakers, we would be safe, as we could
ride almost any wave coming from our backs.

We headed in a northwesterly direction, mostly out to sea as I endeavored to get beyond the boundary of the rocks, which lay just below the surface. The breakers were nearly six feet high now, and we were taking water over the gunwales steadily. We dared not take our eyes from the kicking spray ahead of us, where, we knew, lay the end of the reef.

"I'm out far enough," I thought, "and here we go north," and I swung the nose of the canoe. Out of the corner of my eye, I could see the coming waves, which lifted us up and down, each time throwing us farther ahead. Paddling was very hard and trying to steer in that wind and water was tiring on the muscles of my arms and stomach.

Now we were beside the rocks, I judged. At that moment a great wall of water lifted the stern high into the air and as it ran along the bottom of the canoe, spray pouring in, Walt yelled, "Paddle! Paddle! The rocks!"

Our blades tore furiously at the water and we stayed on the crest of the roller for several seconds, long enough for it to carry us directly over the reef, which we glimpsed beneath us. My judgment had been imperfect, and only that wave, coming when it did, saved our lives. Behind the reef, we drifted calmly, weak from the experience. Had we crashed, we would certainly have drowned. Despite the fact that both of us were good swimmers (we had been on the school swimming team) we would not have lived long, weighted down by heavy boots in a heavy sea.

According to the map that was Observation Point, and later we listened to many stories of its deadliness.

All of that day was not unpleasant, however, for later we came across a crew of white men, working on a dredge in Manigotogan Bay, near a small reservation, and we had a long conversation and two pieces of lemon pie apiece. The tug captain, named Clemons, asked us to greet his brother who was a trader at Port Nelson, on Hudson Bay.

We made a short jump over to Black Island, one end of which was suffering from a heavy fire, to make a search for blueberries. But here our luck failed us.

Coasting in a paradise of picturesque, rocky

pine-clad islands, we saw our first exhibition of canoe paddling, à la Cree Indian. It was a surprise.

Swinging long, crude, hand-made paddles, the two men sat on small cross boards, exerting all their energy on deep strokes, during which they grunted heavily and jerked back and forth. One or two strokes on one side and they would swing the paddle in an upward arc to the other side. Their craft was as long as ours, but wider and much heavier.

Morning dawned cold and blustery. The wind blew from the distant horizon where the choppy waves met the dull skyline. Paddling was difficult because of the wind's direction, and half a day of it, sliding in among reefs and taking wave after wave over the gunwale was enough. At noon we ran into a little cove. One poncho spread over the packs and the grub box had kept our outfit dry, but the few miles of progress were not worth the killing labor.

At last we had been forced to lay up. How long it would last we could only guess. We had talked a lot about how we would enjoy any time spent on shore, fishing, hunting, reading and eating berries. But we were too restless to have any fun. We tried fishing and hunting with no success. Then we read a little and washed some clothes. But we couldn't keep our minds on anything and always wound up pacing the shore, our hands in our pockets, scanning the sky and wishing we could be on our way.

As I wandered along the rocky beach, I caught a glimpse of two Indians in a canoe, coming toward us, expertly picking their way among the reefs. We had seen no one in that direction for the last twenty miles. A bit troubled about their intentions, we slid our canoe into the brush and lay waiting out of sight.

But they passed by, their canoe, evidently empty because it rode very high, taking the breakers admirably. We had the shock of our lives, when, peering from our nook, we saw a large scow, laden with Indian children, weaving along behind the first boat. A huge square sail which flapped crazily kept them going steadily. An old squaw, seated cross-legged in the stern, steered with a paddle.

We felt humiliated. "Darn it," Walt said in disgust, "if they can do it we can." But the day was nearly gone and so we decided to continue our rest.

Crossing Monkman Bay in the morning we asked our direction of two Crees who floated behind a sail in a red canoe. We had seen them further south, either sailing or running an outboard motor. Probably they had trapped all the long, cold winter and then spent their money for gas, which cost about fifty cents a gallon here. They lazed away the summer in typical Cree fashion. While talking with them we saw a big, gray timber wolf on the shore. Catching sight of us it slunk rapidly away.

Here the lake grew narrow and we could easily see across it. As we approached Doghead Point, where a fire was just dying out, we came up through the Narrows, where the water is not more than four miles across. At its widest, it is about seventy miles. The eight-mile jump from Doghead to Rabbit Point we made easily, the water, strangely, as smooth as glass. Even the customary swell was not apparent. Distant islands appeared as a mirage, their trees showing up first, as though the trunks grew directly upon the water. It was warm and at several rock clusters we stopped, stripped off our trunks and plunged in for a swim.

At Rabbit Point we saw a pack of yelping, bloodthirsty, but beautiful, husky dogs. How different they were from the quiet, tame, passive creatures we knew! Their covering was fur, not hair. We didn't land for we noticed their yelping eagerness to reach us—and not to lick our hands, either.

Ducks and geese are plentiful in this region and when we could get close enough we tried a shot or two with our little gun.

At daybreak we were up, resolved to make Berens River before night, or break a few arms in the attempt. It was more than forty miles. When we had left the Winnipeg Canoe Club, experts had given us two weeks to make Berens River, which, because of the uneven shoreline is two-thirds of the paddling distance up the lake. It was 8 P.M. when we stretched our cramped legs on ground again, but when we did, we were in the harbor of the Berens River settlement. Counting our half-day lay-up, we had made it in exactly one week's paddling from the club.

Some kind of a record had been hung up.

## CHAPTER VIII

# *THE ROYAL NORTHWEST MOUNTED*

As we entered the harbor, filled with islands and rocks, we drew up alongside a big boat in which an Indian was fishing. He was short and stocky, dressed in black trousers and moccasins, covered with rubbers, as was the summer custom. He looked astonishingly like a white man and spoke almost perfect English. His name was Willie Everett and, we later learned, he was pure Cree. He knew English because his father as well as himself had been a "Hudson Bay Indian" or a "tripper," an Indian who works solely for the company, on the trail most of the time.

Willie was our constant companion during our stay at Berens River. At supper that night, on a small island to which he directed us, he sat cross-legged beside us, drank our tea and ate our chocolate. Between puffs on his big pipe, he told us stories of the "bush country," stories that kept us awake many hours, despite the fact that we were very tired.

As we lay in our blankets, knowing that several hundred people were around us, but knowing not a thing about the place we were in, we watched the flashing, colored northern lights, which sometimes extended far to the south. And somewhere, on the dark mainland, people were playing a phonograph. The music floated across the bay to us and made us feel comfortable inside.

The light of the gray dawn revealed across the water a low, square, white building, trimmed with red—the Hudson Bay post of Berens River. It was the first of the several posts that grew to be havens of rest and information for us. The "company" store in each district is the center of all official life and the gathering place of natives and whites alike from the several hundred square miles of trapping, hunting, and prospecting wilderness that it serves. The Hudson Bay men, together with the Mounted Police, hold absolute rule over the northland.

Herb Cowan had given us a letter to the post

Indian settlement on lower Lake Winnipeg.

Where the Red River empties into Lake Winnipeg.

Hudson Bay buildings at Berens River. Lake Winnipeg in background.
(Royal Canadian Air Force photograph.)

Air view of Warren's Landing, north end of Lake Winnipeg.
(Royal Canadian Air Force photograph.)

manager. He was away. We met, however, the two young "clarks," as the assistants are known, although much of their labor is making trips by dog team or canoe, freighting flour and other necessities.

In the company of Willie Everett, who was all dressed up for Sunday, we followed the twisting, well-beaten paths through the settlement and strolled among the tiny, mud-calked cabins in which the Crees lived. We strolled at a slow pace, while Willie described to us the varieties of spruce and pine around us and expounded at length upon the soothing effects of balsam pitch when applied to a cut or bruise—something we remembered.

We were walking directly behind a group of six or seven young Indian girls with their mother. They spoke among themselves in Cree, at the same time laughing and giggling merrily. Walt and I couldn't help but feel uncomfortable, since we were certain they were directing their humor at us with our peculiar boots and hats and breeches, but Willie said they were just remarking upon the excellent odor from his pipe. They were wishing they could have a smoke. They all smoke, even the old women and the little children.

After they had switched off on another path, we could hear them whistling loudly, although we could not see them. According to our guide, they were whistling for us, but our inclination to follow them was absolutely at zero.

It takes many years for a people accustomed to centuries of the wild forest life to completely adopt the customs of civilization. Because Berens River is close to the cities of the south and because the steamers stop regularly, these girls wore the same type of clothes that the city girls wear. But their natural grace had disappeared, hampered by an unnatural apparel. They walked awkwardly in their patent-leather shoes, as though they were flat-footed. They wore their clothing with a stiff erectness; their skirts and blouses were ill-fitting and, indeed, all the beauty that should have been theirs was spoiled.

We had intended to go to church in the Methodist mission building, but the doors were closed when we arrived. On the way Willie stopped several old, lined squaws and chatted with them. Some of them shook hands with us.

"Those are the real old squaws," Willie said. "Look how their toes turn in when they walk. The Indians don't walk like that any more."

Everyone was wearing dress moccasins, low-cut slippers with heavy beading adorning them. During the week, and always when on the trail, they wear the ankle-length footgear which is not so ornate. Most of the men wore some combination of different suits of clothes, for the Sabbath. On the trail they stick to their overall, blue denim cloth which is excellent for summer bush travel, for it is warm, takes a long time to soak through and lasts forever.

One does not have to visit California to see a nudists' colony. There is one in every Indian settlement in Canada, at least as far as the boys from the age of six to twenty are concerned. Of course, they don't go about the camp unclothed, but when they get to the "ol' swimming hole," there's only one way to swim and that's in the "raw." We watched them a while and finally Willie coaxed one into diving for us, for a snapshot. Holding his nose he sprawled through the air like a frog and hit the water, mostly on his stomach. It was strange that boys like that, living near the water all their lives, should be such poor swimmers.

Then we met the chief—Chief Berens himself, ruler over some three hundred Crees. The chief had been elected at the annual treaty time, so Willie informed us. He was to hold the title for three years. So far, he had been on the throne for fifteen years and had no thought of retiring. The trouble was, Willie said sadly, that the chief was such a fiery old reprobate, such a crafty politician, and such a fast talker when anyone had courage enough to oppose him, that he had turned his office into a real dictatorship. To be frank, he said, all the other braves were scared of him.

But the Hudson Bay clerks told us that night that perhaps Willie was just a little envious of the chief's reputation and position. Although Willie did look the more handsome and intelligent and although Willie could speak the better English, the chief was just the sort of man who was needed to handle the sometimes unruly Berens tribe.

Not in his wigwam, surrounded by his squaw and papooses, involved in consultation with his medicine men, did we find the chief. No. He was reclining in a most undignified position in a frayed and dirty hammock, under a tree in his front yard, smoking, not a peace pipe, but a foul, black instrument that moved about between his lips as though it had been there for years and years—and it had. He was very interesting. He shook hands solemnly, asked after our health in a nice manner and chatted with us for a quarter of an hour on many subjects. Yes, he had heard of Minneapolis.

We liked Chief Berens. He bore his position with just the right amount of dignity. He had a fine sense of his place, but I cannot say that of some of the white men and women who stepped off the steamer to stare at the Indians. They gathered about the chief in a circle and asked him silly questions like, "Do you have any papooses?" Some of them actually held out pieces of candy, as though he were a bear in a zoo!

We wandered over to the forestry station and met all the young chaps there, the airplane pilot, the radio operators, the pigeon trainer and the cook. They were a splendid bunch. All of them young and strong and intelligent. The more we traveled the more we discovered that it is the young white men that rule the north. Up in an elevated box roost strutted a score or more of beautiful carrier pigeons. One man spends his entire time training them. Every time a plane went out on fire patrol, on a mapping flight or for any purpose, a pair of birds went along in a cage. Two are carried, because sometimes a hawk will get one of them.

Just a few days before we reached Berens River the seaplane there had been forced to land on a little isolated lake far in the wilderness. Both pigeons got back with the news of a broken propeller, Winnipeg was radioed, a plane was out with a new propeller and the men were back in the settlement at dusk.

We had been pretty proud of the *Sans Souci,* until these men caught sight of it. She was a big, strong, well-balanced craft, if you were to ask us. But how they laughed when they lifted it.

"How could you come so far in a little cockleshell like that?" one of them asked.

As they were inspecting our boat and slim little paddles, another fellow strode up and said, "Say, let me try her once." He wore no shirt and never have I seen such well-developed arms, or such a big chest on a moderate-sized man.

He tried the *Sans Souci,* with one of our paddles. It was as though he had a motor on the end. Across the bay and through the reeds the canoe shot like a racing boat. Walt and I just looked at each other. We had developed a pretty good opinion of our own ability by that time, but we were babes compared with this man. As he rammed her prow high up in the mud with one thrust of the blade, one of the "clarks" leaned over and whispered to us, "He's a Mountie."

Well, that explained it!

Private Alfred Jones was the first "Mountie" we had ever met. I had read about them, dreamed about them since I was a little kid, and had ached to meet one in the flesh. That was the biggest thrill I had received from meeting anyone since the time I shook hands with Jack Dempsey himself, and swore I wouldn't wash my right hand for a week. We also met Jones' superior officer and partner in Berens River law enforcement, Corporal Hugh Stewart. The next day we had lunch with the latter in his little house.

Neither was very talkative, but the corporal finally told us how he had taken two unruly Crees from Berens River, across the lake to a railway station, and thence to Winnipeg, all alone in the dead of winter. It was a trip of several days.

"Why, how could you sleep?" we asked him.

"Well, I guess I didn't—much," was all he would say about it.

Our ninth story for the *Star* we wrote late at night in the company office, with a mounted policeman on one side, Hudson Bay clerks on the other, and a few trappers and Crees and half-breeds scattered about, watching the curious-looking white boys manipulate a clumsy typewriter by the light of candles. Plenty of inspiration!

Before we went back to our blankets the clerks gave us a block of black pemmican, made from seal meat. As Walt wrote in the story, "It looks like chocolate, smells like limburger cheese, and has a taste all its own." We hid it far down in the grub box.

In our scribbled diary for the next day, the entry begins, "Went over to the log cabin inn. Met Betty Kemp, the owner's daughter."

Betty, our own age, tanned by the Manitoba sun, was a perfect companion for tramping about the settlement and swimming at her own private little beach. Many were the delightful hours we spent dangling our bare legs from a smooth shelf of granite into the cool waters, munching handfuls of rich, fat sand cherries, practically every bush of which Betty had mapped out.

"Won't you go swimming with me tonight?" she asked. "In June I made a vow to take a dip at midnight every night until school begins and I have to go back to Winnipeg. So far I haven't missed once."

At midnight—brrr! It was the twenty-fifth of August and we were about two hundred miles, as the crow flies, north of the Canadian border. And oh, how cold those August nights would get!

"I feel a bad cold coming on," I protested lamely, and shivered once more at the thought of it.

"Don't mind him," Walt told her grandly. "I'd be glad to go with you."

"Very well," I said, "have a good time." But I was thinking, "Don't expect any sympathy from me afterwards and don't expect any more than your share of the blankets, either, you would-be-Eskimo."

While I played phonograph records at the inn to keep myself awake, they had their swim under the northern lights. Five minutes after I heard the first splash near the rocks before the inn, Walt came into the room, shaking and blue with frost, grabbed a towel and, between vigorous motions with the cloth, stuttered, "That'll be all f-for m-m-me. Anyway, you snickering hyena, I was b-brave enough t-t-to try it." I drowned out the phonograph with my mirth.

Walt and I had planned to start the final stretch of the Lake Winnipeg paddle after his swim that night. Heavy northwest winds had forbade all thought of pushing off during the last two days, and Corporal Stewart had suggested we try night traveling for a while, as the turbulent waters seemed to quiet somewhat at sundown.

As we tightened the last strap on our packs, within the inn, one of the men put his hand on my shoulder and said, "Listen."

We were motionless. Then through the trees

came the small sound of the sighing wind. Gradually it grew louder, like a siren coming nearer.

With stunning suddenness a storm, a northwestern gale struck the settlement. The wind howled and the shutters of the inn banged and clattered. Frequent jagged streaks of lightning, followed by thunder which reverberated through the darkened forest, illuminated row upon row of ghastly white billows, far out on the lake, crashing toward the shore. At last all the tales of sudden death on Lake Winnipeg had been confirmed.

The thought of being out there in the canoe made me turn pale.

## CHAPTER IX

# HUMILIATION OF THE "SANS SOUCI"

HAD Walt not agreed to take Betty's dare of a freezing midnight plunge, the Minneapolis-to-Hudson Bay expedition would have been but a pile of wreckage, washed up on the rocks next morning. This was another indication of something we came to realize many times before we reached home, that the God who guides the footsteps of errant fools most certainly was riding on the weathered prow of the *Sans Souci.*

Very early in the morning, so we would not have to go through a long painful period of saying good-by to our new but close friends, we set out. We paddled to the outer fringe of the countless small rocky islands that cluster in Berens Bay and there stopped for a few hours of much needed sleep. Curling up in our ponchos on a smooth ledge of rock, we soon drifted away to slumber.

I awoke around noon, sitting up suddenly, as a sleeper startled from a nightmare. I felt unusually depressed. My mind seemed to be vainly groping for something which had stood out clearly in my sleep. All that remained now was a clutching feeling of fear—fear of something.

I did not awaken Walt, but pulled on my boots and stumbled up a rocky incline to the island's summit, where I could look out on the lake. During our rest, the north wind had blown stronger, until now it whipped with chilling force through the shrubby trees. Foam-tipped billows curled with resounding crashes on the rocks at my feet. Snipes and sea gulls screamed as they circled and dipped over my head.

Something was speaking strongly in my brain, "You can't do it, don't try. You've licked Winnipeg so far. Don't wreck everything on a gamble now, when you haven't a chance."

Some would call it a "hunch." Whatever it was, it was too strong for me. I stared out over

105

the pitching water for a long time. Another day of wind. It was impossible to get out of the bay, around the long Sandy Point, which stretched another mile to the northwest. Even if we did get out, we could not buck against the five-foot billows. We could ride with them as we had done all the way up the lake, but trying to paddle against them would have only one result and we knew it.

Now I remembered the warning of the grizzled tug commander in Manigotogan Bay, "The north winds are about due to start and then you won't get a foot further up the lake in that shell." We had had three days of north winds now, without let-up.

We could not afford to lay up on shore for days at a time. The seaplane pilot at Berens River had informed us with a sympathetic grin that it had snowed heavily on him once in York Factory the first week in September. Freeze-up was due very soon, and to be caught in the wilderness between Norway House and Hudson Bay would mean only one thing—with our summer clothes and outfit we would never get out. And, too, if we could complete the trip in a hurry, Walt still had a chance to get back home in time for his scholarship.

I confess I wanted to lie down on the rocks and cry.

There was only one logical thing to do—wait two days for the steamer, *Wolverine,* and ride it to Norway House overnight. We would skip but one hundred and fifty miles of the most uninteresting shoreline of the lake, a long straight stretch with hardly a bay. These winds were very likely to blow for two weeks without cessation, and we still had five hundred miles to paddle after reaching the upper end of the lake.

I waited until Walt awoke and then told him my reasons for believing we should take the *Wolverine.* He reacted as I had expected—was hotly indignant at the thought of our letting the lake get the better of us, but I was convinced I was right.

"All right," he said after a silence, "let's flip a coin, as we said we would if we became deadlocked on anything."

The steamer won.

In the end, I was proved to be right, for up to the time we reached Norway House the lake was in a constant state of roughness, with the wind always from the north.

Back into the sheltered bay we coasted, almost ashamed to meet our friends and hear them say, "Why didn't you believe us when we told you you couldn't get out?"

For the next two days, Walt and I loafed— just loafed. We made the rounds of the settlement upon succeeding invitations from the Hudson Bay people, the priest, the forest-patrol men and the Mounted Police. I am afraid if it had continued much longer we never would have been able to convince our appetites that we must go back to our own cooking.

Occasionally Walt and Betty went swimming in the lagoons, but as my swimming suit was tattered beyond respectability, I often dozed on the warm sand, trying to entertain six-year-old Dickie, Betty's little brother. I am afraid my talk with Dickie went too far. I carelessly assured him that we would be glad to take him to Norway House with us. So one morning before we were dressed, he showed up, dragging his toy suitcase, and announced importantly, "Let's get going, boys."

Now another problem raised its head. We had very little money left, although we expected a check from the *Star* when and if we reached York Factory. Passage on the steamer as well as freight charges for our canoe would amount to about ten dollars each, we were informed. Ten dollars apiece was all we had.

When the *Wolverine* or the "Wolf" as the freighter-passenger is more familiarly known, jarred to a stop at the long log dock of the Hudson Bay Company, Walt and I took the bull by the horns and marched up to the purser. He was swell. When we started to mention our financial status, he interrupted with, "Oh yes, Mr. Jones here tells me you boys are a little up against it. Well, I think we can arrange it for about five dollars each—that will include your meals."

Good old Jones! He had got wind of our troubles and had waylaid the purser, Mr. Shepherd, and made some sort of plea for us. I hope he did not pay the balance out of his own pocket.

Into the side of the ship we piled the *Sans Souci*. What a comedown for our tough little boat—riding in the belly of another ship, one that could manage the waves when she could not.

109

Dinner was being served as we embarked. Watching Berens River fade away as the forest closed over the settlement was fascinating, but so was dinner. Dinner got most of our attention. We sat next to a missionary, the Reverend Walters, who, with his wife and charming little daughter, was on his way back to his little church at Norway House. When he learned of our trip and destination, he promised to give us letters to the Archdeacon at York Factory.

Eating noisily on our other side was a trapper, prospector, trader and general man-about-the-woods. He was tall and thin, and his red hair had the appearance of having gone uncut for months. He talked incessantly—of himself. When we mentioned our seven-day trip from the city to Berens River, he said, "Why me and a partner I used to have come up from Winnipeg and reached Berens in *five* days. And furthermore, we had ten hundred (a thousand pounds) of flour with us. And another thing, we went up the west side of the lake and then cut across, a whole day's jump, in nothing but a canoe." He said he was a graduate of McGill College. According to his story he had the most beautiful wife in the north,

110

but wouldn't subject her to the hardships of his cabin life.

Later we learned that his tale of making Berens River in five days was untrue, that he had never been near McGill College, and that he had kept his poor wife out in the bush for so many years it had broken her in body and spirit. He turned out to be the only bad egg we found in the large basket of the north we explored.

After dinner I climbed to the top deck of the "Wolf." The dying sun, a huge blood-red disk, tinted deeply the low-hanging western clouds; and on the heavy waves the blood of the sun seemed to be sprayed, enchanting each white billow which leaped and rolled with its brothers in a crimson sea. It was a gorgeous spectacle and as I stood clutching the forward rail, moving rhythmically with the rolling motion of the boat, I felt something of the urge which turns sailors' faces always toward the water. I felt a sense of power over the strong, crafty lake that I had never known before. This was different. One could learn to love a body of water like surging Winnipeg, roaming on a ship like this. There would not be that eternal fear of the lake's smashing strength which helps to determine your every move when you travel in a small craft.

Gradually, in the dimming, low-lying mass which was the shore, we lost sight of the indentation which we knew was Berens River. The last dark island slid away. The mantle of gray which misted the waves grew into lapping blackness. My hands which clung to the rail felt a moist chill grow upon them. The *Wolverine* swung due north and pointed her dipping and rising nose toward the polar star.

Low voices speaking in the old tongue of the American savage floated down from the pilot house, accompanied by intermittent puffs of tobacco smoke. The half-breed navigators were settling down to the night of silent, watchful steering. As I pulled my sweater closer and turned to descend, I caught a glimpse of their glistening, yellow-brown faces and their gleaming eyes as they strained to pierce with their vision the fog of the night ahead, into which the ship was slowly coasting.

> "... and a grey mist on the sea's face,
> And a grey dawn breaking."

Dawn "broke" through my porthole, chased the gloom of the night up and down the walls and flooded over the white sheet that covered me in my little bunk. Morning at sea! (At least I could imagine it was the sea.) Memories of our departure rushed back upon me and out I leaped, eager to catch sight of the land which would betoken the beginning of the wilderness into which we must plunge, for five hundred miles, to the northeast.

But there was Walt, ahead of me, perched on the rail, gazing ahead. We seemed almost on top of the long wide point of land that ran out from the western shore, still hidden in misty fog, out into the swelling lake and across our bow. Somewhere, a few miles to the north of this point, Warren's Landing, lay the settlement of Norway House.

## CHAPTER X

## "*THE DIE IS CAST*"

"To Hudson Bay, eh? Well, boys, hate to discourage you after coming so far, but I don't think you can do it. Be gittin' pretty cold now in a couple weeks and I'd hate to see you get froze up way out in the bush somewheres."

I didn't look up at the speaker, a fisherman who watched us load the canoe for the short run from Warren's Landing to Norway House, until I was sure the bailing can was wedged tightly in the prow. I tried to grin at him. No use arguing about it any more; these people were convinced one way, and we were convinced another.

Twenty-five miles to the settlement, they told us. "Watch for the side current because here is where the lake empties out and becomes the Nelson River. And keep your eyes open for the wooden markers. Watch the reefs, because she's going to blow hard this morning." Advice was plentiful, and very necessary, at this point.

We swept off into the maze of islands.

"Bud," Walt said, without turning from his position in the bow.

"What?"

"Know what lake this is?"

"Sure, Playgreen Lake."

"Remember what the women in the Parliament building told us about the government party up here last year. How they knew this lake and yet were lost for two weeks. Remember what she said about the name coming from 'plague-of-a-lake'?"

I remembered. "What of it?"

Walt turned and grinned. "Attaboy. I'm not scared either."

We felt better then and harangued a while on the general uselessness of government officials in canoes, anyway. Oh, we were cocky fools, all right, but the luck of fools seemed to be with us.

By and by, the west wind piled the waves higher and higher and we rolled the boat more perilously to escape them. A cold rain began to fall and, for one of the first times, I felt chilled clear through. Dipping the paddle, uncertain whether a mounting wave would run up our soaked arms or not, trying to bail, trying to keep our slickers around us, trying to watch the rollers, trying to follow the markers on the islands—we were rapidly becoming miserable. An aching pain crept into my cold legs to complete the anguish.

After a while I broke the silence by saying, "We haven't seen a marker for a long time, Walt."

He did not answer. He knew it and didn't want me to worry, so he had kept quiet. We paddled on, skirting islands. They all looked alike and sometimes I felt sure that we were going in a circle. Blessed of the Gods that we were, our luck held, however, for suddenly we saw a fisherman, sitting on a big motorboat, beached in the lee of an island.

He stood open-mouthed as we swept by atop the piling breakers.

"Too rough! Too rough! Come in!" he yelled through cupped hands.

"No!" we screamed back, above the crash of the waves. "Where's the outlet?"

"There!" he pointed. "The white rock!"

At noon, as a big red seaplane roared out

116

Air view of fort at Norway House—where we began our 500 mile wilderness jump. (Royal Canadian Air Force photograph.)

A glimpse of God's Lake and the many islands.

The start of a fishing trip at God's Lake.

Camp at evening. Bud dries out the fishing line.

across the narrow channel of the Nelson River, carrying the famous Ken Durwar, forest-patrol pilot, we slid along the plane's dock before the Norway House fort, to be greeted by a chorus of softly sworn ejaculations from a group of wet and soiled aviators, as they read, "Minneapolis to Hudson Bay" emblazoned below the gunwale of the *Sans Souci.*

Well, we had done it again. We had given the treacherous Playgreen Lake a decisive licking— with the help of the fisherman.

Not a glimmer of satisfaction penetrated my aching head. Here we were, squatting before a square of low, log-constructed, red-topped buildings, every one of them at least a century old. It was the famous Norway House fort, several times the scene of Cree attacks since the first daring Hudson Bay men, or the "Company of Gentlemen Adventurers," had penetrated the incredible distance from the bay to Lake Winnipeg and from there down into what is now the United States.

Dramatic history fairly cried out for recognition all around us. We squatted, cold and wet, the center of a questioning circle of Mounties, aviators, forest-patrol men, Indians, trappers and traders, all wanting to know how in the world we thought we could get to the bay before freeze-up.

Not a thrill of pride was I conscious of. All I could think about was dry clothes and a fire, a fire and dry clothes.

Directed to Playgreen Inn, we clumped past the wreck of a long, clumsy scow as big as a miniature yacht. Not until I was curled before the fireplace at the inn did it occur to me that what I had seen was a York boat. Think of it, a York boat! One of the crude contraptions first nailed together at York Factory, in which traveled eleven trappers at a time, hauling it over the many Nelson River portages on log rollers. Here was the flintlock, Indian-fighting past rising up in front of me and I was stepping aside to let it pass.

We were off!

Five hundred miles beyond, across a vast stretch of wilderness, lay our goal, the North Atlantic Ocean. Could we do it?

Laden with food enough for nearly a month,

twice as much as we thought we should need, we pushed off from the fort dock, while overalled and moccasined Cree braves, fat squaws and gurgling Indian babies, stared at us, and the white men and women cheered.

I was trembling a little, I confess. Walt, in the bow, sat stiffly erect and paddled hard, without a backward glance. It was frightening to cut off all communication, all connection with these people. Unconsciously, we had been morally bolstered by their presence during our two-day visit at Norway House, and now we struck out, without knowing when or where we would see the next white person, realizing we had just an equal chance of getting through the wilderness to the bay without getting hopelessly lost in the intertwining rivers and lakes or without getting caught by the sudden freeze-up. This was hard to grin away.

We had not elaborated on the dangers that lay ahead, in the story for the *Star*, which was taken out by plane through the courtesy of pilot Bob Nevins, for that would have scared our folks to death.

Could we do it? We had to, for there could be

no turning back, once we had left Norway House. We never could paddle back up any of the swift rivers that cascade to the bay, and hiking through the dense, impenetrable "bush country" couldn't be done. Suppose we smashed up our canoe in a rapid and lost our outfit, our food, our blankets and our matches and rifles—what then? If we actually did make our way back to Norway House we would be no better off. The steamers would have ceased running then. We would have no money. A check from the newspaper might await us at York Factory, and ninety miles back up the Nelson River from Hudson Bay was the new Hudson Bay railroad. That was our only chance.

The proprietor of Playgreen Inn, Mr. Lowe, had given us a supply of grub, equal to that which we were expecting to arrive by steamer from Winnipeg, shipped by a Canoe Club member. We had traveled faster than anticipated, however, and had to make this arrangement, as we could not wait for the ship bearing our supplies.

Our route to the bay was to be via God's Lake and God's River. It was not the regular route; indeed we could find no one who ever had paddled the entire length of that river. Trappers, Mounties, Indians—everyone always went by the Hayes River, which had been a famous route for more than a century. But at the inn we had met Karl Sherman, a young, ruddy-faced Norwegian trapper, who, in his twelve years there, had learned to know nearly every stream of any consequence in the region.

"The Hayes is low now," he said, "and it might mean days of wading and dragging your canoe. The God's River is full of bad rapids and the portages are tough, as far as I have gone, to Sucker Creek, but from there it is clear sailing, I am told. The Sucker Creek rapid is tough and has no portage. If you don't know much about rapids, you'd better learn before you hit *that* one."

We took his advice against all the others, for somehow he inspired confidence immediately. I think Sherman was about the hardiest man I ever knew. Instead of sticking around the posts all winter, putting out a few traps near by, he was the kind of man who would run trap lines two hundred miles long and sleep on the trail all winter.

121

"And if you boys don't send me a wireless by September twentieth, telling me you're safe, then I am to wire the *Minneapolis Star* that you are lost out in the bush—is that right?"

We nodded. The speaker was Mr. Ashton, young wireless operator for the Royal Canadian Air Force at Norway House. We had stopped at Forestry Island, a mile from the fort itself, before slipping out of Little Playgreen Lake into the "bush." This was the last day of August. We should make York Factory in two weeks, we were positive—surely in twenty days.

The next day, slipping rapidly along the coursing Nelson, we stopped at the sight of a white man, very young, squatting before a fire on the shore, surrounded by Crees. It was raining and we were glad of a little warmth and conversation. "Let's stop," Walt said, grinning, "they might be the last human beings we'll ever see."

Nice, cheerful thought.

The white man was a fire ranger; the Crees were his crew. And not a very willing crew either. Usually when they fought fires, they received two dollars a day, but this fire was on an island which was part of the reservation. So their chief just drafted them and they labored for nothing—except maybe the chance to shoot a moose now and then.

Bill Watkins, the ranger, told us many stories about the Crees and gave us a newly baked bannock, or Cree frying-pan bread, a pound of butter, a tin of jam and half a pound of tea. We remonstrated.

"Aw, that's all right," he assured us. "We get it from the government anyway, and there's no end of it lying around here."

As a parting favor, Bill, after a few expert shots, adjusted perfectly the front sight of our .22 rifle, so that after that we were able to make many meals of partridges, ducks and snipes. Our sights had been off line entirely.

Bannock, they told us, will ruin a white man's stomach in two years, if he isn't careful. It is much too heavy for regular use. Walt knows all about it. He must have thought he had to show the fire ranger the very depths of his appreciation, for he ate at least half a bannock himself. What a tummy that boy had at night. He groaned and rolled all night. In the cold, drizzling morning, Walt was pale and a trifle shaky, but better. He guessed he had used too much butter, so he gave that to me. On second thought, he guessed he would keep our brown sugar, since I had the butter—the Shylock!

Watching the maps we had obtained from Ashton, which were detailed, but unmarked, we swung due east at the High Rock, an immense granite mass, shaped like a huge loaf of bread and covered with tiny pines. Now we were in the Echimamish River, pronounced "Itchy-momish." That means, in Cree, "water that runs two ways." Try to figure that one out! Well, a couple of days' paddling down the tiny stream, one comes to the "height of land," a divide. There is a dry portage of two hundred yards, then more water, which is supposed to flow east. In reality, there is no current on either side.

"Bud!" Walt yelled suddenly from the stern.

I almost fell out of the canoe twisting around. It was another one of Walt's ideas, this time a good one.

"Just feel the breeze behind us. Why don't we put up a sail?"

Out we piled, into the willows and cut a stout pole. Our square sail was an entire poncho, which

is bigger than the average blanket, and the sail,
I must admit, was very crude and very hard to
manage. But it worked. With one of our crew
of two scrunched down in the bow, bracing the
mast, and the other "ruddering" with a paddle
under one arm and the other arm wound about
the sail ropes, we skimmed along nicely.

Curled in the bow, I watched the unending willows slide by, outlined against the unchanging
gray horizon. Occasionally rain pattered down
on my slicker. On we sailed and I fell asleep.

The sound of voices and the grating of our
gunwale against another drew me out of my
dream.

A heavy, gray, Indian-freighter canoe, an old
Chestnut, occupied by a middle-aged Cree, two
Cree children and a white man, and powered by a
battered two-cylinder outboard motor, was alongside. The children were pointing at the funny sail
and grinning. The old Cree stared steadily, the
inscrutable expression in his black eyes, which
were enfolded by wrinkled flesh, remaining unchanged.

But it was the white man in the bow, talking
earnestly with Walt, who held my interest. His

hair, which straggled from under an old-fashioned hat of city make, was sodden gray and his unkempt beard was gray, but his weak blue eyes were those of a young man.

He spoke eagerly, almost with the enthusiasm of a child. After years in the wilds, laboring in the service of the Lord at the little mission on Island Lake, this priest was on his way to Norway House, where he would put the children to school and himself embark for Winnipeg and eventually for Quebec, his home. "Going out" at last. There was no doubt that we were the first whites he had seen since the start of this happy return journey, and all his pent-up emotion flowed out in expressions of joy.

So this was what the men had meant by "half-bushed." Neither this clergyman's sensitive mind nor his delicate physique had been meant for the bush country. Constant association with stolid savages, the grim loneliness of long winters had chafed the fine edges of the former; heavy bannock, greasy fried meats and back-breaking portages had destroyed the latter.

Later we learned the priest was thirty-five years old. We had guessed his age at least twenty years more than that. Either one masters the northland, as Karl Sherman had mastered it, or one is mastered, as our poor priest—there is no compromise.

## CHAPTER XI

# CANOEING WITH THE CREE

WE were lost—no doubt about it. We sat and stared at each other as the sweat ran into our eyes. On our maps there showed no indication of the reedy lake which circled away before us. The Echimamish had meandered into this body of water and despite two careful rounds of the shore line, we could find no outlet. The beautifully fringed lake smiled on in the September sunshine, while our despair grew.

Immediately, various thoughts filled my panic-stricken mind: failure of our trip . . . the end of our grub . . . despair at home . . . searching parties. The tendency to curse myself, the north country, our own foolhardiness, was growing, but with a mental wrench I resolved to be calm, to try to work quietly with Walt in evolving some plan of action.

After some study of the intricate map system and frequent consultation with the compass, we decided we had left the Echimamish and had wandered up some one of the many streams which enter it. But which? Then we thought back. "Your next portage is three miles on," the priest had informed us, the day before, and we had made the next portage. After that point, now that we recalled it, we *had* seemed to swing more to the north than to the east. So back we went, fifteen miles to the portage, painful traveling, combining paddling with wading in soft mud and dragging the canoe.

As twilight slipped through the spruce, we came upon it. Sure enough, the correct water trail flowed to the right and continued on, and did not, as we had supposed, form a little lagoon, so frequent below falls. From the description given us by the priest, we had assumed naturally that this falls was the site of our portage, and we had made it. Immediately around the bend we found a waterfall almost identical with the first. The second was the real place for our portage.

The misspent day of paddling was not an entire loss, however, for Walter, the sharpshooter, picked off a fat black duck at one hundred yards.

The prow of the *Sans Souci* nosed silently through the water of the narrow stream hour after hour, and the willows thinned out, then vanished, and with growing thickness, spruce, jackpine and balsam grew in their stead. Through Hairy Lake we pushed, appropriately named, for tall reeds choked the surface.

On a slab of rock we saw a freighter canoe, tipped over a complete outfit, apparently the property of an Indian. It lay in open view, easy booty for any thief. But we knew it would not be touched. That is one of the unwritten laws of the north. You may as well shoot a man as steal his outfit from him in the bush country. It means death, a slow and torturesome one.

Then, suddenly, we found ourselves in the midst of desolation. Fire, the scourge of the pine country, had swept through an immense area along the Echimamish on both sides of the stream, only a few days before we appeared on the scene.

With our big black sail, flapping like a scarecrow, leading the little craft along the stream, between row on row of black trees grim in their deathlike silence, the picture must have been bizarre, in the nature of a nightmare. Flakes of ash soiled the surface of the river, caught on the prow of the boat and hung on in thin gray lines. I thought of Browning's poem, "Childe Roland to the Dark Tower Came." Long after sunset we swung the paddles, until the acrid smell of burnt wood faded and green grass and moss grew again under trees that were alive. Then we camped.

"At this rate," Walt was saying one morning as I sprinkled a little sand in the tin plates in a half-hearted attempt at washing dishes for the ten thousandth (more or less) time, "we'll get to York Factory in time for Christmas dinner. What we should have done was to invest in two pairs of skates."

He wasn't far wrong. The nights were cold. In the morning, the black rubber poncho on top of our blankets would be white with frost.

One noon I sat on my felt hat, as if it hadn't taken enough punishment, and when I eventually arose it was a mass of wrinkles and was quite shapeless. That night I punched out the crown to approximately the correct contours and set it on the ground. In the morning I picked it up with a cry of triumph, for the cold had set it firm again and not a wrinkle was visible. Walt washed his socks one evening and hung them over the bow of the canoe. When we arose, they were heavy with clinging icy particles.

As we thought of the significance of these things for the hundredth time, the creak of wooden oarlocks reached our ears. Excited, I stood gripping a dirty breakfast plate as a big canoe, manned by two Indians and carrying a white man who sat reading in the center, swirled around the bend.

At a word from the white in Cree, the Indians, one rowing in the bow with clumsy, homemade oars, the other swinging a paddle vigorously in the stern, put into shore at our feet.

"My word," the white man exclaimed, "is this all the progress you have made?"

Ashamed as we were to admit the fact that we had lost the trail, we were greatly relieved at seeing the man. We soon recognized him as Ralph Butchart, the young clerk in the Hudson Bay store at Norway House, who now was on his way to God's Lake to become manager of that post.

Ralph invited us to travel along with him and his "savages" as far as his destination. "With that little canoe," he said, "you should keep up with us very easily."

Nearly bursting with joy, we flung everything into our boat and shoved off, to trail the big boat and its three occupants. And for four days after that we trailed them.

It was a gorgeous experience, living with the Crees and this experienced woodsman, but it almost broke our backs to keep up with them. We paddled as fast as they, because they had three hundred pounds of flour with them besides their regular equipment and all Ralph's worldly goods —but oh, those portages!

In the first place, our canoe could not be carried by one of us. The middle thwart was missing, we had no portage yoke and our paddles were not long enough to serve as shoulder braces. Each portage meant two trips apiece for us. First we would load each other up with about one hundred and fifty pounds of outfit and stagger the distance. Gasping, we hurried back and threw the canoe to our shoulders.

There seemed to be something about each

133

portage that put frenzy in the hearts of the Indians. Within two minutes after beaching they would have about two hundred and fifty pounds apiece on their backs, and away they trotted as though their very lives depended upon speed. And Ralph always took an immense load, too, supported only by a tump line across his forehead.

It was then we found all the things wrong with our outfit. Our pack sacks were too small, our wooden grub box had no straps on it and handling our box of hard tack was like holding a slippery fish.

Our Cree friends were named Moses Gore and James Robertson. Many Indians have biblical names, given by the missionaries. Moses was fifty-four years old and yet he could portage the heart right out of Walt and me. Jimmy was in his twenties and, unlike Moses, would not talk with us in English. I don't think we said four words to him during all our journey and he never said one to us.

A tump line is a very neat little thing, but I hate the mention of it. I am horribly prejudiced, of course. The strap resulted in a sensation in my neck like hanging from the gallows all day. I

Bud essays a difficult portage with pack held by tump-line.

Lunch with our Indian companions. Moses and Jimmy in the center, Walt at right, washing dishes.

Pow-is-tick Rapids on the Nelson River, north of Norway House, which we avoided by our route to the Bay.

could hardly turn my head one way or the other after trying the tump once. But it is true, of course, that once he's used to it, a man can support more weight on his neck than anywhere else.

We simply had to keep up with our friends. We did, but what a cost! At night we could not eat; every muscle was aching. While Ralph tried to be consoling, yet grinning over his tin cup of tea, Walt and I gave each other muscular massages and found some relief. Good-natured Moses laughed aloud each time we groaned, and as for Jimmy he said nothing, as usual.

Ralph was a prince. At night when we were able to sit with our backs to a log and let the heat of the long fire the Indians made thaw us out, we had long talks together. Ralph was Scotch, like most Hudson Bay men. We were surprised to hear that he was a college graduate, extremely well read and, under the rough exterior one almost has to adopt in the far north, gentle and refined. He thought our trip was the greatest thing he had ever heard of, and told us so. Of course our hearts warmed toward the tall, slender, red-headed northerner more than ever.

Ralph had two more years of service with the

company and then his term would be up. He told us he wanted to go back to Scotland and live in a city again, but constant reference to this thing and that thing which one must learn "to be a good bushman" showed us that he was growing closer and closer to the northland in his heart.

Each morning, when it was yet dark, the rough hand of Moses awoke us. There he would stand, shivering in the flickering light of the growing fire, wearing a childish skull cap which he always slept in. Breakfast for Moses and Jimmy usually was boiled rabbit. Jimmy caught a bunny nearly every night in a little snare of cord which he would loop over a rabbit trail.

We would paddle and portage steadily until noon, when we stopped to "boil the kettle." Then, until about five o'clock, we again labored, without a lull. After our supper at five, we took the trail once more and kept on until dark. Never did we camp except in a portage spot, where these Indians had spent many nights before. Sometimes we found supplies of fuel, already cut.

Our course followed a long chain of miniature lakes which lay close together and yet unconnected. Crystal clear, very cold, these gems of water lay deep in valleys of granite and row on row of pine and autumn birch reflected in their depths. Over these hills of rock we had to carry our outfits.

With our own inadequate maps, Walt and I would have wasted hours, searching for the portages. Twice we followed the canoe ahead into what looked like a blank granite wall. The men in the leading craft seemed to melt into the hill. Each time, following the bubbles they left, we came upon tiny channels which led to the portage start.

Moses instructed us in the making of a sail for our canoe. It consisted of only two spruce poles. One, the heavier, was chained upright in the bow, acting as the mast. The other, one end of which hung in a flexible loop by the side of the mast, halfway up, formed an angle to the mast, the whole effect something like the letter Y. The sail, again our poncho, stood out squarely to one side of the mast. Ropes were tied at the top and bottom loose corners of the sheet, and we had a genuine Cree sail.

But we were more daring than wise with our sailing. The poncho was much bigger than the piece of canvas used by the Indians and, as our craft was lighter, the effect was thrilling—and almost disastrous. On the first sailing attempt, Moses steered out upon little Lake Robinson, after we portaged away from the Echimamish. We watched Moses handle his ropes. Their boat slid along so nicely, so smoothly, that Ralph took out a book and began to read. Then we pushed off and paddled out into the wind.

Wow! With a groan the mast leaned far over and almost snapped as the stiff breeze caught the bellying poncho. The *Sans Souci* creaked in surprise and tipped abruptly to the sail side as we threw our weight to the opposite gunwale. Like a frightened loon, our canoe bore down upon the jabbering Indians and astonished Ralph. Past them, missing by inches, we swirled, the bow almost under water.

"Take it down! You'll swamp!" Ralph yelled.

Take it down indeed! As easy as handling a runaway moose in a cyclone. Besides, it was exciting fun and as soon as we saw that we could keep upright, we did a little experimenting with the sail ropes. We found we could sail splendidly with a side wind, and even tack.

That had Moses and Jimmy beaten. It took a strong side wind for them to move and, for fancy things like heading at an angle into the wind, that was beyond their landlubberish comprehensions. Oh, we were sailormen in the grand style for a while! Our stock rose immeasurably in the eyes of the Crees.

Since meeting Ralph and the two Crees we had seen no other persons until we met another group of Crees going toward Norway House. Canoe over our heads, we were feeling our way along a portage trail. I was in the rear and could see a few feet farther ahead than Walt. A pair of moccasins came into view, padding toward us. I assumed it was either Moses or Jimmy returning for another load, but I could not see higher than the man's knees.

Suddenly there was a crash. My forehead banged the stern thwart. Walt went down on his knees as though he had been shot. When my head cleared a moment later, I was on the ground, also. Elegant Cree curses were crackling through the frosty air. When we got the canoe off our heads, there was an Indian, whom we had never seen before, staggering to his feet, by the side of a big freighter canoe. He had seen our boots coming, but not our canoe, nor had we seen his boat. Consequently, the prows of both craft met squarely, with almost stunning force. The man was in a rage, but gradually it dawned on him that our coloring was simply sunburn and that we were white. He shut up like a clam, hoisted up the canoe and went on without another word.

When Ralph heard how we had tried to put on a jousting act with canoes, he lay down on the grass and howled.

## CHAPTER XII

## GOD'S COUNTRY

ONE night a party of Indians from God's Lake met us as we were camping. Except for looking us over curiously, they did not try to become acquainted. After supper, Moses and Jimmy joined the group about their fire in a talk which lasted until we were ready for bed. As we were drifting to sleep, we heard the voices of all of them raised in a murmurous chant.

"Their prayers," Ralph whispered to us from his bed roll. "Always say them out loud."

In the morning, Walt and I watched them make the portage. A boy about sixteen years old trotted away over the quarter-mile portage with a very heavy canoe on his back. True, he could not get it up on his shoulders alone, but he made the run entirely unassisted. Carrying things on their shoulders and necks seems to be born in the Indian children. Later we saw a boy

141

about ten years old stagger up a steep hill with one hundred pounds of flour on his back, without stopping a minute for rest.

That afternoon Walt and I had a new experience—we helped fight a forest fire. Well, maybe "fight" isn't the word, as we just dug a crooked ditch around a smoldering area of stumps and rotting wood. It was on the shore of Lake Aswapiswanan. Apparently somebody's fire had not been put out properly and if the keen eye of Moses had not noticed the thin curl of smoke arising into the clear morning air, a disastrous fire would surely have resulted.

When we picked up our digging tools again, Moses made a long blaze on a balsam and with charcoal wrote something in Cree, the characters resembling those in Chinese writing; but he did not tell us what the meaning was.

Then something happened which seemed a catastrophe at the time—we lost the Indians and Ralph.

We had caught some fish trolling from the canoe and had taken a little extra time at supper to cook them. Touchwood Lake lay but two miles ahead and we agreed to rejoin the other party on

142

the biggest island, as they did not wish to wait until we finished our meal. So they went on. The shadows were growing long as we pushed out on the lake. In the increasing darkness the water was black and we lost the outlines of several islands ahead as dusk fell. We strained our eyes anxiously, watching for the flicker of a flame.

There was no sign. Islands slid by us, huge black forms in the night. Now it was impossible to distinguish the chosen one. We camped, hoping that by an early start we could catch the men before they entered the channel which connected Touchwood with God's Lake.

Dawn came, bringing with it a stiff wind which blew cold rain particles into our faces. A dense fog shut out the landscape like a gray curtain. But we could do nothing but push ahead. Now our ability as navigators was really put to a test. Newspapers back home had said we were "intrepid." Now we had to prove it to ourselves.

According to our map, Touchwood Lake stretched away for twenty miles in a "dogleg" fashion. It was filled with islands and the shore line we followed was so indented with bays and peninsulas that without careful checking we could not tell whether we were actually following the shore or merely winding in among islands.

We set the compass on a thwart and steered our course, counting our paddle strokes carefully to check our mileage. By noon the fog had lifted considerably. We ate an anxious lunch of cold beans. Finally we decided we were opposite the spot where the outlet should be. We searched among the bays for an hour.

Then Walt said excitedly: "Look, Bud. There must be current here. See how the grass on the bottom bends that way?"

This bay did not look hopeful, but suddenly, turning a corner of a small island and pushing through heavy reeds, our boat picked up speed and we shot into a stiff current which carried us straight at the shore. The mass of granite parted and we were on the river. Safe!

Inspecting them carefully first, we ran two rapids and coasted out on the beautiful expanse of God's Lake as the barking of dogs announced the warming fact that we were among human beings again. I cannot imagine how a lake could be more thrillingly beautiful than God's Lake. No wonder that name—God's country, indeed.

Such sights as this are reserved for those who will suffer to behold them. The clear, calm level of the lake stretched as far as our eyes could see and, like precious stones in a setting of silver, islets reflected the afternoon sun in splotches of color. The air was blue, so blue, as though the sky had settled down to earth.

Before dark we found the post, tucked away on an island miles up the lake. Immortalized by Curwood in his story, "Nomads of the North," it was one of the shrines of the north country to us. We landed in the face of a growing crowd of curious Crees who knew when we were yet far away that we were white, because of the steady manner in which we paddled. Ralph broke through the circle with a cry of welcome.

"At first I thought I should wait for you when you didn't show up," he said, "but then I figured maybe it would be good experience for what lies ahead of you. If you fellows can navigate through that stretch, you can go anywhere."

Cheering words!

The log post store was about fifty years old, one of the oldest in north-central Canada, while thirty yards away, in a clearing, stood the manager's home, a four-room frame building of drab, faded coloring. Here, as we were stretching our tired legs and warming our hands, we heard a commotion outside. Mr. Henry, the post manager and his clerk, Ernest Barton, known as "Jock" like all company apprentices, had beached their motorboat, home from a fishing trip. They were playing a game with three Indian squaws. But what a game! Ernest and Mr. Henry, with terrible war whoops, threw huge fish at the squaws, who screamed in delight and flung them back with vigor. This probably would have gone on until the whole settlement was embroiled in a grand piscatorial battle had not the eyes of Henry finally caught sight of three strange white men surveying the proceedings.

For he did not know Ralph Butchart, either, nor was he acquainted with the fact that Ralph carried orders making himself manager of God's Lake and transferring Henry to Bloodvein River, on southern Lake Winnipeg. The company does things abruptly. Giving the two men time to have their conference, we reëntered the house, to see Henry bending over a map. He had his finger on the Bloodvein. "Holy Smoke!" he

146

Part of the Indian settlement at God's Lake.

Trading post at God's Lake.
Left to right—Butchart, Barton, Solomon, Henry, and Indians.

A Cree boy demonstrates for us with his bow and arrow.

Typical Indian scene at God's Lake.

exclaimed. "Almost back to civilization. Well, if they've got a good team of dogs, it won't be so bad."

The fact that he had just had a change in bosses did not affect Ernest, it appeared. Henry, while a great musher, was just a little eccentric and difficult to live with, Ernest confided. Bullet holes dotting the walls inside the house testified grimly to his peculiar habit of letting fire whenever he chose. The skull of a man atop a case filled with books, which were almost falling apart from much reading during the dark winters, was riddled with shots. It had been there for many years, Ernest told us.

"Just one taken off Skull Island. Many years ago an epidemic killed off most of the inhabitants here and all the bodies were moved to an island somewhere in the lake. Except for the man who brought back this skull for proof, no one ever has found the island."

To people who sit comfortably before their fireplaces, with all "the comforts of home" around them, visions of snow-swept forests, clouds of mosquitoes and monotonous daily fare keep them from admitting that there actually can exist

147

a "spell" in the north for anyone who has known real comfort. If ever there was proof that these people are wrong, Ernest Barton was it.

Here was a young man of twenty, well educated, affable, a good athlete, born and reared in London. Hungry for adventure, he had signed up with the company. After a year, God's Lake was home to him. "Oh," he said, "I go out to Winnipeg occasionally, but after two or three days I'm sick of the noise and dirt and soft living and petty talk. This is real life here."

There is a cleanliness, a breadth and sweep and strength in the north, a purifying realization that one is living close to the fundamental elements of life. Yes, the north has a spell.

The three Hudson Bay men, Walt and I and "Donald," a half-breed whom they "figure a white," sat about the dining-room table that night. Walt and I listened as they smoked and talked of their experiences.

"Oh, things are quiet enough among the savages," Mr. Henry was saying, "unless somebody starts a rumpus like Joe Trout last winter. Joe, a talkative old fellow, had the village believing he was a medicine man. So the sergeant—he hasn't been around for some time—told Joe he would have to prove his ability. Joe tried to get out of it, said he wasn't feeling well and that white men didn't understand the spirits, anyway. But the sergeant just said, 'Joe, you and I are going over on another island alone tonight and if you can make medicine for me you'll be the prima donna around here the rest of your days. But—if you can't make medicine, you've got to go to every tepee and tell them you are a fool.' Joe stamped and chanted and made funny passes and drew marks in the snow with full moonlight to coax the spirits near, but the sergeant, who probably is stupid and not in tune with the infinite, sat on a stump and sucked his pipe in silence, and saw no medicine. So Joe was humbled in the eyes of his friends forever after."

"Say," Walt spoke up after a while, "why was it all those children laughed at us when we walked up the pier with our fish?"

Walt was proud of those fish, which weighed about seven pounds apiece. He had hooked them trolling on the way to the post, and when they were pointed at with fingers of scorn by several dozen Cree youngsters, his pride, his fishing pride, which goes far back in the Port family, was hurt.

"What kind of fish were they?" Ernest asked.

"Northern pike."

"No wonder they laughed!" And the men proceeded to laugh also. "We call them jackfish. They go to the dogs for winter grub. People around here eat nothing but whitefish. Of course, when there comes a famine, they'll eat jackfish, but not until then. Don't let the kids see you eat them. Better throw them to the pups outside. We have a nice mess of whitefish if you must have fish to eat."

Throw to the dogs those glorious, shining, fresh-water monsters, the biggest he had ever caught! Not Walt. And to show him I was thoroughly in sympathy with him, I helped him eat the jackfish.

The "pups outside" were a team of five beautiful, square-headed gray huskies, easily the most powerful and handsome dogs we saw anywhere. What a difference between the ordinary canine playmate and these gigantic brutes! The grace with which they sprang for the fish heads we tossed to them, the suddenness with which they crushed the food with one snap made us realize that these were not dogs useful just as pets and as innocuous companions for children—these were animals with a purpose, the most highly prized possession a northerner may have.

"How much," Walt queried, a trace of red creeping up from his collar, "are those candy bars?"

We stood before the log counter in the post store, packed and ready to hit the trail after a comfortable night's sleep on the kitchen floor in Ralph's new home.

"Two for a quarter," answered Ernest. "Oh, don't look surprised. Things get higher priced than that out here in the bush. One winter, flour went up to twenty-five dollars a hundred and gasoline for motorboats usually is around two and a half dollars a gallon."

I drew out our entire money supply—exactly two dollars and five cents. But those luscious, bulging bars of sweetness, what memories of the corner drug store they brought back! I looked at Walt; he looked at me. We both gulped.

"Er, we'll take, er, four apiece," I said, and

151

Cæsar could have felt no more emotion when he crossed the Rubicon. One-half of our finances blasted! But we had had many weeks without sweets and we couldn't help it.

"Well, boys, good-by and God take care of you," Ralph said to us as we stood up in our canoe and shook his hand.

The last tie with safety was being broken. More than three hundred miles of practically unexplored wilderness lay before us, down a river traversed, perhaps, by only a handful of white men in history, never covered by any of the whites or Crees we had met so far.

"I don't know anything about the rapids, but the current should be very fast and I think you should make York in about eight days," Ralph went on. "What do you think, Solomon?" he added, turning to the Cree tripper for the post.

Solomon scratched his head. "Dunno, nev been down God's. Tink maybe ten days, lots rain soon now."

## CHAPTER XIII

# *THE GREAT TEST*

WATCHING the wavering needle of the compass we pulled the blades through the crystal water with all our strength, like racing horses, straining and eager, down the home stretch. We wound in and about among hundreds of islands, until noon, again counting our strokes in order to know at every minute how far we had come.

"Head for the nearest tip of Elk Island," were the words of Ernest which reverberated in our brains. "You could never tell when you hit it except for the fact that it has just been burned over."

We were to follow Elk Island eastward to the other tip. After that it meant a dash straight across the twenty-mile breadth of the lake, aiming toward the outlet into the God's River.

At noon we hit the end of an island still smoking and black from recent flames. With each mile along its shore we became more and more confident that this was Elk Island, the largest in the lake, according to our photographic map loaned to us by Karl Sherman.

Great masses of gray clouds blotted out the stars that night as we camped on the beach, eager for the new adventures we anticipated on the river, if we could find it. Sherman had put amazing trust in our ability to get to York, but even he had advised a guide to find the river. Well, we had taken our chances alone again. Could we do it?

Morning dawned cold and blustery. Map outspread, we set the compass. Our course must be straight to the quarter of a mile. Indeed, that far to the east and we would be in a part of the lake and of Manitoba which never had been charted. The airplane map extended no further eastward than the exact line on which we traveled. The sensation was much like sitting, safe, in a glass cage and looking out into something wild and unknown and dangerous. Not far to the east, we knew, lay the province of Ontario.

We steered onward, straight north now, speaking little and concentrating intently on our

154

course. Should we lose our position now, it might easily mean we never would regain it, for islands are so confusing when they are grouped by hundreds and even thousands. And to find our way back to the post seemed pretty hopeless.

At last a long wall of forest confronted us. Perhaps another island, and yet the terrain rose too gradually to the height on which the spruce grew, the forest spread out to the northward in such solid waves! No near-by island could be this large, according to our map, or else we had lost our course. We beached and lunched and for dessert munched happily our treasured bars of sweets.

Half a mile westward and suddenly we were in a strong current. Again we had done it! And missed the river only by half a mile!

"Mr. Sevareid," said Walt pompously, extending his hand like an archduke, "I congratulate you, rawther splendid you know."

"Sir Port, positively gorgeous. You, my lord, not I, deserve the plaudits of these gaping multitudes."

But only the spruce and the birch could witness our triumph.

Let the clouds glower! Let the sun frown behind the mask of mist. We were warm inside with the glory of personal achievement and the sensation of safety. Into the churning river we raced, yelling like wild men, cheering the river on to more and more speed. This was traveling! No more lakes, no more islands to worry about, nothing but straight going now. Nothing to do but follow the gurgling river, riding like kings on the current.

So we thought then. It was not long before we learned differently.

By nightfall our shoulders ached from continual portaging. Our first night on the river, we camped with the roar of a long, broken waterfall lulling our slumber. We awoke in a drenching, frigid rain, our blankets, even between the ponchos, soaked, our clothing which had become uncovered, also soaked.

There is nothing more disagreeable than a wringing wet forest in cold weather, unless it is paddling a canoe in cold rain. So that day we constructed drying racks and dried out the clothes and blankets, spending our time fishing. Before night we fixed up a stew which was to last several

156

days. This was the combination: jackfish and beans. What a mess! But we had learned to like everything.

We wasted that day because we thought we had plenty of time, now that we were on the right trail. But we soon learned that we could never stop any more just because of rain, or we would not get out of the bush, for it rained continually.

We added to our troubles when Walt broke his paddle as it wedged between two rocks. It was my fault; I chose a shortcut out of a little lake formed by the river and we ran suddenly into shallowness. Now we had no extra paddle. If we broke another we would be helpless. I felt rotten all that day.

Within the next few days we became expert at running rapids of all descriptions, and there are hundreds of varieties. We *had* to become expert. Searching for the faint portages, unused for months, or hacking out a new portage as we did several times, took hours and hours of valuable time. So we ran most of the rapids.

The roar would come to our ears shortly before the maelstrom came into view. The stern man, who must assume the greatest responsibility, would rise to his feet as we drifted swiftly toward the leaping white water. He would choose the best route among the rocks, the best line of kicking riffles to follow. He would give his directions and then, paddling with all our might, to get up more speed than the current itself, we would drive the *Sans Souci* (poor, worn-out old boat that hadn't hoped to die in such wild surroundings) straight at the dashing foam.

The daily drizzling rain and the foggy mist that accompanied it made the always dangerous task of running rapids still more dangerous. Often we were forced to put into shore, then get out to examine carefully a mist-hidden rapid, stumbling and slipping on the rocks which were sheeted with frozen sleet.

A hundred times we scraped with sickening sound on the black boulders, a hundred times the canoe shuddered violently as though about to fall in pieces when we rammed into shallow ledges, a hundred times the bobbing prow was submerged and a rush of icy water flooded our outfit. A whirling gash in the water meant a rock anywhere from five to fifteen feet up stream from it.

We learned to judge the size and depth of rocks by the nature of the riffles they caused.

Your speed must be greater than that of the current, or you will have no leverage to twist and throw the canoe from one angle to another. The bow man must slip to one knee and lean forward, paddle poised, in readiness to get the blade between the boulders and the frail craft.

We had not paddled long one morning when a far-distant rumbling like thunder reached our ears. Half an hour went by and the noise increased to a great roar but still we had not come upon its cause. At each bend we almost dreaded to look down the ensuing stretch of water, afraid of what we were going to see. At length we came to it, and when we did we were forced to shout in each other's ears in order to compare observations.

The God's River had amazingly narrowed to about one-quarter of its normal width and was pouring with raging force like a horizontal cataract through a narrow gorge, between huge slabs of granite.

There was no possibility of portaging around the place with the canoe without spending at least two days clearing a path. But our packs we could take, and did—after struggling with the underbrush for two hours. Then we removed all our heavy outside clothing and unlaced our boots so they could be slipped off in a moment if necessary. In the middle of the emptied canoe we placed a flat rock, weighing about one hundred pounds. We were ready to try it.

Into the gorge we shot, tossed like a feather on the five-foot riffles. We were helpless to do anything but try to keep the canoe straightened out. Thrusting a paddle into those waters was like offering a toothpick to Niagara Falls. Spray struck us like a rain squall. In five seconds we were through the worst, but still going at incredible speed, and straight ahead loomed a wall of rock which shunted the river to right angles. Sideways we swirled toward the wall, paddling desperately to follow the current before we hit.

"Can't make it!" Walt gasped. "Your paddle!"

The wall was upon us. Crack!

The canoe shook as though hit with a catapult. It tipped precariously, swung upright. It was the copper tips of our paddles that had struck the wall. Had the gunwale hit, the boat would have

160

Falls on God's River which we did *not* run. Wonderful trout fishing here.

One of the many rapids on God's River which we *did* run.

Walt with grub box on top of the load, starts
a portage on God's River.

Halfbreeds, all dressed up for Sunday, at the corrugated tin church
at York Factory.

crumpled like matchwood. My heart was pounding wildly and my legs shook under me as we stepped out on shore again. I looked at my paddle. The stout copper band on the end was twisted and torn, ruined for further use. Walt's was somewhat the same, but our paddles had not broken.

Sometimes long shallow stretches forced us to get out and wade in our boots, which now no longer kept out the water. We had to wade for more than half a mile at times, through ice cold water, and our legs were numb for hours afterwards.

Drip . . . drip . . . drip.

Every time we touched a branch, drops showered upon us. Twenty yards of pushing through the trees and we were drenched again. Now even birch bark refused to burn readily. Dry wood was impossible to find; only by painstakingly cutting out heart wood could we start a fire. We laid our blankets close to the fire, usually with a lean-to above us. Vainly we would try to dry our clothing. By the time it was half fit for wear, our eyes, aching from smoke and weariness would refuse to stay open. We never failed to awake in pouring rain. Sleep lasted but a few hours each night. The dark hours were dreadfully cold.

Each day we scanned the skies anxiously, watching for a break in the clouds. But day after day the leaden heavens lowered above. The icy wind blew directly against us time and again. Our faces grew raw and black from exposure. We could not shave, nor even wash our faces. All our wearing apparel was on our backs, day and night. We lost the heels to our rubber-bottom boots and walking over slippery rocks with the canoe over our heads was very dangerous. Once, as we were pulling the canoe along by a rope, Walt slipped and slid backwards down a twelve-foot granite wall. Like a cat, he landed in the center of the boat and by a miracle he did not tip it.

Our conversation consisted of nothing but opinions as to where we were, as to the length of time our food would hold out, of good meals we had once eaten, of warm beds we had once slept in. Hour upon hour we talked of these things. Problems of our former life suddenly appeared petty, ridiculous, laughable. Worry about marks at school, about shows and dances, about athletics

—what were those things now? Good food and dry clothing and warm beds, that was all life held, we were sure.

One day we came to a long falls. To the right a little stream entered. This must be Red Sucker Creek, we thought. So, according to directions, we wrapped up Sherman's map, tied it on a stick and stuck the stick upright between two rocks. We felt better then, for now the river would bend east and soon we would run into the Shamattawa settlement, where there would be Indians, if no whites.

But as the river, fringed by green banks of spruce and dotted with yellowing birch and poplar, continued to run steadily to the north, we became worried. Walt remembered Sherman had said there was no portage at Red Sucker, and at this place we had found one. Then we were wrong. Just where could we be?

Sick about our slow progress, we still considered it necessary to stop and catch the rainbow trout that swarmed below the many waterfalls. For we must augment our rations or they would not last. We determined to eat only a certain

163

small amount each day. Our sugar gave out—a loss much more serious than it sounds. Then we ran out of hard tack. But we still had pancake flour and with it we fried a good supply of the little cakes each night and ate them cold the next day in place of the hard-tack biscuits. We quit the practice of making a fire at noon, in order to save time, and knew no warmth from dawn until nightfall.

The animals stayed well away from the river, hidden in their retreats, for the fly time was past. We saw only a wolf, a black bear and occasionally smaller animals. In an attempt at diversion, we chased a loon two miles along the river one day. One night we sat upright, startled out of sleep by the unearthly scream of a lynx close at hand. We gripped the rifle and waited. But the scream was not repeated, only a low rumbling sound came to our ears and then ceased. Another morning, when we got up, we found the deep impressions of a giant moose in the clay of the river bank. The animal had come to drink that night, only twenty feet from our camp.

The thin gloves on our hands rotted away and there was no sensation in our fingers as they gripped the paddles. Our frozen hands could not perform the delicate operation of skinning slippery trout. So we held the fish in our teeth, while our wooden fingers directed the knives.

The portages were overgrown. It was evident that no one had gone through the region for many months. Our canoe began to leak badly. As I was pouring water over the breakfast fire one morning, I saw Walt bending over and peering intently at something in the water of the river. When he beckoned to me, there was a queer look on his face.

In a quiet pool, tiny, weblike traceries of shore ice were forming.

But enough of physical misery. We went through mental torture, too. I hate to talk about that, but it is something that most travelers in the wilderness must go through. The story is an old one to men who live in the north.

Slowly, the unending monotony of the forest gloom, the cold, depressing misty half-light in which we traveled and the unceasing discomforts we underwent, began to fray our nerves. Gradually our dispositions gave way under the strain. We became surly and irritable. The slightest mishap set our nerves jumping. A sudden blast of wind against us, the upsetting of a dish of food, the refusal of wood to burn—these little irritants put us into a rage. Impossible as it appears to us now, we began to vent our ugly moods upon each other, to blame and accuse for things we would have laughed at two weeks earlier. At first all this went on only in our minds, but each knew the other's thoughts and it was only a matter of time before it came to words. Like children, we bickered.

And then we came to blows. One cold morning, as we prepared to load the canoe, a trifling incident occurred which now I cannot even remember. Something in our minds snapped, our moral strength broke down. We leaped at each other. Hitting and twisting violently as though we were fighting for our lives, we rolled over and over until we struck a tree trunk.

The same thought must have come to each of us at the same moment and we were sane enough to recognize it in our separate minds: separation here in the wilderness would mean but one thing —death to both. We needed each other as much as we needed food to eat and water to drink.

166

Without speaking a word, we released our holds, staring at each other as if we had been having a bad dream.

Then we loaded the canoe and set out. My eyes were fastened for hours at the back of his head, as he sat in the bow. He did not turn and I spoke no word. All morning I felt no emotion of anger, nor of sorrow, nor of forgiveness. My mind was numb with the awfulness of it and I could not think.

At noon we came upon a great stream which burst like a thunderstorm into the river. I believed it must be the Shamattawa, but there was no sign of a trading post. A curl of smoke arose high on the hill. We clambered slowly, avoiding each other's eyes. If there had been others around we would have been brought to our senses. There was no one; only a forest fire dying under a rotten stump. We climbed down.

There was no portage to be found and we waded and dragged the canoe until we could stand the cold water no longer. Then we crawled into the trees halfway up the cliff, out of the frosty wind which drove the rain into our faces. There we ate a can of cold beans, shivering and crouching to escape the wind. We wore the beaten looks of despair. Some sort of pride prevented us from begging each other's forgiveness. A grip of the hand was all that was needed, but somehow it did not occur.

Along a ridge of slippery rocks we made an improvised portage of one hundred yards, canoe over our heads, leaden feet sliding carefully along the narrow route. A slip, and a plunge of fifty feet into the river below would follow. But on that day danger made no impression upon my mind. We completed the portage.

The river turned east and we knew we had just passed Red Sucker Creek. We were far behind our schedule. Our misery was complete. We put up the tent and made a bed of spruce boughs.

In the midafternoon of the next day, as we skirted a bend, my eyes fell upon the remains of a camp fire. My throat choked with excitement as I tried to cry out—for the ashes still smoldered! Tense with expectation, we drove the canoe rapidly around the next bend and strained our sight down a long stretch of water. There! Two miles ahead, a large dot was unmistakably moving. We paddled with all our strength, yet it was two hours before we were within hailing distance.

It was a canoe filled with a Cree family. In the stern the father paddled, his pipe gripped between his teeth. In the bottom of the boat, at his feet, sat the squaw and she also paddled. In the middle of the canoe, snuggled among sleeping bags, a stove, a tent and boxes, guns and bundles, were three little children, the two nearest the gunwales helping with sawed-off paddles. In the bow sat a girl of about sixteen, and she was paddling also. Along the right bank trotted their dogs, two mongrel hounds.

In normal states of mind, the sight would have been ludicrous, but we did not laugh. We were so glad to see them. They ceased paddling as we drew alongside. We pointed to the water which slipped between the two canoes and asked, "God's River? Shamattawa?" In answer to all our questions, they nodded their heads and smiled. That did us no good.

Then Walt started to "talk" sign language. I think he was trying to ask how many days would dawn before we came to Shamattawa, if this was still the God's River. He looked so funny, waving his arms about before the puzzled Indians, that I burst into laughter, despite myself.

Walt stared quickly at me, flushed deep red under his brown, then fell into laughter with me. It was as though a strong wall between us had crumpled into nothingness. At that moment something glorious happened—the sun broke through the dull clouds and the river and valley turned to gold as its warm rays flooded everywhere, burnishing the yellowing poplars and lighting up the stolid faces of the Indian children.

I did not see the expressions upon the countenances of the Indians as Walt stretched over the packs and gripped my hand, because my eyes were blurry and I seemed to be melting inside.

The squaw was pointing to my watch pocket. I took out the watch. She took it, scrutinized it carefully, then motioned me to look. Her brown finger pointed to five-thirty o'clock, and she said, "Shmattwa." It was now almost five. Only half an hour away!

As we ran a small rapid, thumbing our noses at it joyfully, and coasted out onto the new river, the Shamattawa tepees came into view. "The company?" we yelled at a Cree repairing a net on the bank. He pointed. We hadn't dared to hope for it—but there, running down the steep embankment to greet us, were two white men!

## CHAPTER XIV

# *VICTORY—AND PINEAPPLE*

Jock Third and Walter Gordon, Hudson Bay men, had come to the post this early in order to build a little frame house. No one visited the place except in the trapping season. Now they bundled us into their cabin and, sensing our exhaustion, ordered Indians to carry our belongings up the hill.

They brought us hot water to wash and shave. Hot water! Think of it! And, as we turned from the wash basin with sighs of happiness, we found a huge supper waiting us. Oatmeal, bannock, bacon, *johnny cake,* butter and jam! The men watched from their seats as we ate eagerly, almost like starved men, and they laughed heartily at our antics. Hours later, with the good feel of warm boards under our backs, we drifted peacefully to slumber, the heavenly music of a battered phonograph dying out of our minds.

"No, you're not through with rapids yet," Jock

said the next morning as we prepared to set out on the one hundred and twenty miles that remained between us and York Factory. "There's one more, about twenty miles down. It's two miles long. Run it on the right side and you should get through—although the Indians themselves sometimes crack up in it."

A cheerful thought to start the day!

"You boys should make York in two days. That is sixty miles a day, but the Shamattawa is one of the fastest rivers in the world, considering the fact it's half a mile wide. After you hit the Hayes, it's faster going yet."

One dollar remained in our wallet. With half of it we bought a pound of hard tack, so big and heavy it took but six of the biscuits to make a pound.

Waving to the white men and the handful of Crees who stood on the shore, we pushed out into the stream. What a stream it was!

"Shamattawa" means, in Cree, "fast-running water." It was very shallow and four feet below us the rocks slid by in a blur of speed. Had we chosen to drift without using the paddles we would have made fair progress.

173

Now Jock had said to run the rapid on the right side. We did. But he must have had a slip of the tongue, for later we found that the left side was the correct one. You can guess the result. Here is what our daily notes say about the episode and the rest of the day:

"Twenty miles down we hit a two-mile rapid, which we ran at terrific speed. It was one ridge of rocks after another, miniature waterfalls. Twice we jammed to a dead stop and twice we hit such big riffles the canoe shipped several gallons. As we hung on one ridge, we could feel the boat begin to crack. Bud got one foot out and shoved us off, before the canoe went to pieces. Longest and toughest rapid yet, and our last. Stopped, dried out our stuff (a sunny, fine day). Repaired the rents in the boat. Shot a ptarmigan. Paddled four miles more and camped. About ninety-five miles to York."

Walt was in the stern on that never-to-be-forgotten day, and it was a masterful job of steering that he did through that rapid.

Stuffed with the fresh meat, we lay and watched the glorious northern lights flash in breath-taking colors across the sky. There was not a cloud. We went to sleep confident that this night there would be no maddening rain.

At dawn we awoke, just as the first dash of a

rainstorm struck our exposed faces. There was nothing to do but get angry with the contrariness of the weather, slip into our slickers, tip up the canoe and shoot off into the speeding current, peering through semi-darkness and downpour to escape the many perplexing shallow stretches in the river.

As the day progressed the rain increased and it grew much colder. We built no fire at noon, and, as we huddled under a tree eating our lunch, several "Whisky Jacks," birds whose real name is We-sa-kay-jac, known as the "camp thieves," fluttered nearer and nearer, attracted by the ptarmigan bones we tossed away. To my surprise one of the birds alighted on my boot, and showing no fear at all pecked the meat from my outstretched fingers. In some settlements, the tameness of these birds is a fatal drawback, for the little Cree children—the meaner ones—catch them, pick out all their feathers except those on the wings, and let them fly away, to freeze to death.

We camped at the junction of the Shamattawa and the Hayes. We looked up the new stream curiously, picturing in our minds our first sight of it, branching off from the Echimamish, very slow and narrow, near Norway House. It had grown in size during its five-hundred-mile trip down the great watershed to the bay.

Of course it was cold. Why, it was sea air we were breathing. The sea! We had never seen it, but now we should before many hours were up. You who have grown up on the coasts can never know the wondering, the dreams about the ocean, that we poor inland unfortunates experience. Just to gaze upon it had been one of my most cherished desires since childhood. And because we foolishly thought the tides would be affected so far up the Hayes, we pulled our canoe well up on the flat, hard, cold bank of clay. The tides! Think of that!

We had no relish for going into the dripping woods, so we camped upon the clay and it was an experience I never shall forget. One of us would keep the fire going by blowing on it, while the other fried cakes, acrid smoke blinding and choking both continually. We would snatch the cakes from the pan, gulp them down, blow on the fire, cough and choke, rub our smarting eyes, gulp some more and huddle closely together to main-

176

tain some warmth. While our faces burned, our backs froze.

We put up the tent and spread the ponchos and blankets directly on the clay. It was like lying on a cake of ice, but we had become so hardened and were so weary that we slept.

Our notes for the next morning read:

"Last day on the trail. Got up at 5:30 A.M. and hopped around in the freezing cold while we ate the last can of beans cold, a few prunes and half a hard tack. Hit the trail at 7. Hands and feet wet and numb. Paddled against strong north wind till noon. Ate last of chocolate, last of prunes, a raw potato and half a biscuit. All out of grub, practically. . . ."

The tremendous Hayes rushed on and on in great long sweeps between limestone cliffs one hundred feet high, and we rushed on with it, putting mile after mile behind us, determined not to stop until York Factory was reached.

Our views were in four- and five-mile stretches now, and we approached each turn breathlessly, straining to see the broad expanse which would mean our long, long trip was ended and our goal accomplished. If our arms ached, we did not know it. Faster and faster we whipped the paddles through the water until the *Sans Souci* seemed to leap at every stroke.

And, suddenly, there it was.

It slid into our pathway, quiet and calm as though it had been awaiting us. The river banks fell away to low marshlands, and water glistened as far as the eye could reach. Straight ahead, several miles away, rode a schooner, silhouetted sharply against the distant horizon.

For a moment I felt very calm. I was not excited. I merely thought, "This is what all the rivers come to. All those rivers. This is the sea, where everything ends."

Then I saw my companion's face, and the import of it finally reached my brain. Why, our trip was over. Yes, think of that. Just think of it—paddling was to end. I could see by Walter's face that he was shouting, but it took a moment for his voice to break through into my brain.

"Bud! Bud! The ocean! The ocean! Wake up, man, wake up! We've done it, we've done it and they said we couldn't!"

Then I shouted too and fell across the packs and grabbed him by the arm, not realizing I was almost upsetting the canoe in the deep water. I was very happy and in a little while I felt very proud, too, so much so that it seemed to be bursting out of me at every pore.

Darkness was creeping down, the schooner was fading away a little and paddling became harder and harder. We knew it was the incoming tide doing that, it was the sea pushing us back toward the wilderness as though trying at the last moment to prevent us from reaching our goal.

In the growing dusk, buildings came into view on the left embankment. This was York Factory, site of the greatest of all trading posts a century ago, port of entry for thousands of pioneers. Here warships of England and France had fought for the great fur country through which we had just come. A few dogs yelped at the sight of us; a few Indians peered curiously over the banks. On we went until the white square of large buildings comprising the company came into view. A few hundred yards away, lights blinked on the schooner.

We stepped out upon solid ground. Our benumbed legs buckled under us and we nearly fell. That day we had paddled the canoe sixty miles in eleven hours. We staggered up the steps and as we strode along the boardwalk, our steps clattering strangely in the stillness of dusk, we shouted at a staring half-breed, "The factor?" He pointed to a sloping little building hidden behind what we assumed was the main storehouse.

Frozen fingers pounded the heavy door. It was jerked open by a tall, heavy-set, mustached man.

"Factor Harding?"

"Right here, I'm him. My word, boys, you're half frozen! Get over here by the fire and get those wet clothes off."

"Factor, we have letters of introduction for you——"

"No need, no need," he answered, brushing the papers away. "I've had letters from Minneapolis here for days waiting for you to arrive. Read all about it in the Winnipeg papers. What a trip you've had!" And he turned to a group of men sitting around the supper table, whom we noticed for the first time.

"Can you imagine it, Reid, these fellows have paddled a canoe all the way from Minnesota, in the States? Why, it must be a couple of thousand miles. But here, you boys must be starved." And he rushed into the kitchen, issuing commands.

180

Unloading the schooner *Fort York* at York Factory.

The great Shamattawa rapid, two miles long, which we ran on the
wrong side. 100 miles from Hudson Bay.

Air view of York Factory where our journey ended. (Royal Canadian Air Force photograph.)

Last resting place of the *Sans Souci*. Our canoe lies face down, on the exact spot we landed.

I cannot amply describe that meal which we gulped between answers to dozens of questions from the puzzled men about the table. Sitting with us were the factor; his assistant, Archie Harkes; Colonel Reid, a Hudson Bay official from London there on an inspection tour; Mc-Donald, post manager on his way to Severn River settlement; and the captain and mate from the schooner, the *Fort York,* here on its annual trip to bring in supplies for the winter.

As we ate, Walt opened the letters that awaited us. Most were from our folks and friends and the majority of these began something like, "If you get this letter you will be alive and not dead out in the wilderness after all."

But, from a practical standpoint, one letter interested us more than all the rest. It was from Mr. Robertson of the *Star,* and said:

"By the time this reaches you, you will have completed your long journey and I want to congratulate you on it. It certainly is quite an exploit and you deserve credit for your courage and tenacity. Inclosed is a check for fifty dollars which concludes the payments we agreed upon. I realize this may come in handy and hope you will soon be back in Minneapolis with nothing but good effects from your long journey."

Short, but oh, so sweet! Broke, we had become millionaires simply by opening a letter. As we were about fifteen hundred miles from home by rail, we were going to need everything we could get.

I halted an enormous chunk of moosemeat on its way to my mouth and said, "Say, how about that little can of pineapple we've saved for our victory dinner? This is the victory dinner, and I'm going for the pineapple."

Laughter ran around the table as I broke off in the middle of the meal and dashed out of the door. And it is a lucky thing I did or we would have lost our canoe and entire outfit. We had pulled it part way up on the sand, forgetting entirely, when we landed, that the tide was coming in. When I got to it, the *Sans Souci* was afloat, its nose shifting about uneasily in the sand. In five minutes it would have drifted out into the current, been carried up the river in the night, and in the early morning hours, when the tide went out, would have floated far out to sea.

Maybe that little tin of fruit had been a luck charm for us all summer. At any rate, we ate it.

Just as we were leaning back in our chairs,

emitting huge sighs of happiness, Factor Harding bustled in and said, "Boys, where's your grub box?"

I had cached it under a piece of canvas, weighted down with rocks, and I told him so.

"Get right down there," he said, "the dogs here are fierce. They will eat through canvas, tin, wood, or anything."

So out I dashed again, Walt along this time. Growls came to us in the darkness as we approached on the run. The dogs were into our outfit! Two rocks missed them, but they scurried away, snarling. The canvas was torn apart, the box tipped over, everything in a mess. A chunk of bacon was still intact, strangely enough, while a box of pancake flour had been devoured. The block of pemmican given us at Berens River also was gone, which enraged Walt.

The dogs at York Factory were particularly fierce and dangerous. They slunk furtively about the buildings, ugly and skeletonlike. When one died he was promptly eaten by the others. Almost the only food they received was the seals which the tide cast up on the shore after the frequent Indian hunting parties. Seal hunting was their favorite sport. In their canoes they would follow the sleek black heads which popped up above water here and there, until close enough for a rifle shot. They made no attempt to retrieve the animals, but left the work to the tides. The fur of these seals is worthless.

## CHAPTER XV

# HALF-BREEDS AND MUSKEG

DURING our two days at York Factory, Factor Harding told us many stories of the north country, in which he had spent all his life since running away to America at the age of seventeen. He had been on the trail with Stefansson, Ernest Thompson Seton, the naturalist and writer, and with many other famous men who have lived in the north.

And he told us a story of dogs, to show us how savage they could be. At one post, the wife of a Mountie had raised from puppyhood a team of dogs of which she was very fond. One day, when her husband was away on patrol, which sometimes lasts many weeks, she made a short trip with her team. By some means she fell and was hurt. It was not long before the entire team of full-grown huskies attacked her, and when an Indian came upon the scene shortly afterwards, the animals had ripped away most of the flesh of one leg.

They carried her to the post. In a brave effort to live, she submitted to amputation of her leg, without anesthetics. The men used a skinning knife and a saw. But poisoning set in and after a few days she died, without seeing her husband. When he returned and learned the story, he seemed to lose his mind. Pulling his revolver, he shot every dog in the place and later quit the police service.

Yes, the dogs are savage, but they remain the most valued animal in the north, and a good team is often worth its weight in gold to the owner. Not all teams are as bad as that one, and indeed, many Mounties, Hudson Bay men and Indians owe their lives to their dogs.

Then we told the Factor a story of the "rune-stone" found in 1898 at Kensington, Minnesota, which is not far from the Red River. It is one of the great treasures of Minnesota at present. The stone was found by a Scandinavian farmer. Chiseled on it, in old Viking language, were the words: "Eight Goths and twenty-two Norwegians upon a journey of discovery from Vin-

186

land westward. We had a camp by two skerries one day's journey north from this stone. We were out fishing one day. When we returned home we found ten men red with blood and dead. A. V. M. save us from evil. Have ten men by the sea to look after our vessels fourteen days' journey from this island. Year 1362."

If the stone is a true relic of the fourteenth century, and most students of Viking history now believe it is, then white men visited the interior of America one hundred and thirty years before Columbus sighted its eastern coast—and, it is quite possible that these Vikings had sailed into Hudson Bay, gone through either the Nelson River, or the Hayes, or the God's River, down Lake Winnipeg and into the Red River.

Perhaps Walter and I had retraced the exact route on which the first European explorers had penetrated America.

Fifteen miles by sea around the point, the majestic Nelson flowed into the bay, at Port Nelson, named, not for the great English admiral as the world supposes, but for the poor mate of a sailing vessel, who died on shipboard and who was buried there, according to the factor.

187

Factor Harding was the only real "factor" we met. Once this name, with all its romantic implications, was given to all post heads, but now these are merely called "post managers." Only after twenty-five years of meritorious service, does a man now receive the coveted title of factor.

Other stories of York he told us. There was one about the famous English author, Robert Ballantyne, who came to York Factory as a boy and served six years there. It was there he began to write. We were shown the original contract the boy signed with the company, a document of great value now.

Walt and I had a bed apiece at night and slept between smooth white sheets.

In the morning, after a refreshing sleep, we decided to go to church with the Crees, for it was Sunday. The church, built of corrugated tin, was about fifty feet long, and its one beauty was a stained-glass window sent from England by a Duchess. The men sat on one side, the women on the other. All were dressed in their most brilliant shawls and in their beaded moccasins. Life is drab enough for them and color is one way to brighten it.

188

Most of this group were half-breeds, but they sang the hymns in fairly good English, if in poor harmony. The archdeacon's wife played the tiny organ up in front, and a young deacon preached a simple sermon. Later he would talk to the full-blooded Crees, using an interpreter. After the service, we approached the deacon's wife and gave her the letters for her husband, from the pastor at Norway House. She accepted them gratefully and told us her husband was then two weeks over-due from a trip to Severn River. I do not know yet if he returned safely.

All kinds of questions from various individuals about Minnesota and the United States in general finally convinced Walt and me that we *were* a long way from home, after all.

"Minneapolis?" Colonel Reid asked. "Where the deuce is Minneapolis?"

And when he wanted to know just why we had made the canoe trip and I answered, "Oh, for pleasure, I guess," he exploded: "Pleasure! What a jolly funny kind of pleasure!" But he amended his statement with, "Oh well, that's youth. Things look different when you're young, I suppose. My word, I almost believe I envy you."

189

The captain of the schooner was sitting in Factor Harding's library also during this conversation. Short and stocky, he had the strongest pair of arms I ever have seen. We saw him push two big Crees out of his way and lift a five-hundred-pound can of gasoline over the gunwale of a skiff. Now he reached for a bottle of whisky and said, "Well, anyhow, let's have a drink in honor of the canoeists."

When Walt and I hesitated, he looked at us quizzically and said, suddenly, "Say, how old are you now, anyway?"

When we admitted our ages, the group seemed to be shocked with surprise and of course their attitude changed. They had thought I was about twenty-five and that Walt was about twenty-three! I guess hardships do things to your face.

Jock Harkes, the clerk, led us into his room in the evening and with a grin uncovered something marvelous—a radio! We begged him to try to catch the Minneapolis stations and he tried hard, but something was wrong and the only signal from home was a faint squeal.

Suddenly Walt whipped the earphones from his head and grabbed my arm, almost shouting.

"Bud! Bud! Yesterday was the twentieth. The twentieth of September and we haven't wired Norway House that we are safe. That means they have sent word to the paper. Maybe they have started a search. Holy Smoke, our folks will be worried to death."

And the tragedy was that York Factory had no equipment to send messages through the air. We imagined our parents, sleepless over our reported disappearance, while here we were, happy and safe, enjoying ourselves. But there was nothing we could do but try to get up the Nelson River ninety miles to the Hudson Bay railroad and get a wire through.

On the heels of that thought came another which struck both of us at the same moment. Walt's scholarship! It was lost. Never in the world could he get to Chicago in order to enroll at the university on time.

We had beaten the wilderness but time had beaten us, and I wondered, for my partner's sake, if the adventure had been worth it. Walter stoutly insisted it had. He tried to hide what he was feeling about his disappointment, but I could see that he was hurt.

191

He pretended anger when I offered sympathy. "Oh, rats, I can always go to college, but how many chances will I ever get to spend another summer like this? I'm not worrying about it, so why should you?"

I didn't bring up the subject again, and he never mentioned it.

We left our battered canoe, most of our ammunition, our tent, fishing outfit, slickers and all but a few light things we could carry on our backs, when we departed from York. We had arrived there just in time to miss a boat going up to "steel," as they call the railroad, and so we had to hire half-breeds to take us back up the Hayes for nine miles, then across a five-mile muskeg portage to the Nelson River and Port Nelson.

We took a last look at the *Sans Souci* resting in the shelter of the river bank, where we had landed. After months of trials which the boat had not been built to undergo, we had become attached to the canoe with something of the sentiment a man feels for a horse or a dog.

Some day, Walter and I will go to York Factory and take the *Sans Souci* home again. The factor promised it would always be in his care.

Before we shook hands with the few white men in the place and clambered aboard a big canoe with two half-breeds, Factor Harding wrote out a letter bearing the seal of the Company, which read as follows:

"To whom it may concern: This is to state that Messrs. W. C. Port and A. E. Sevareid of Minneapolis, U. S. A., have come from their home town, paddling their 18 foot canoe all the way to York Factory, via Winnipeg, Norway House and God's Lake. It is a remarkable journey for two lads to make without guides. This is the first time this trip has ever been made, being a distance of about 2,250 miles.
(Signed)  C. HARDING."

The trail home!

Portaging through five miles of muskeg swamp is something I shall remember to the day of my death. Instead of having the guides take our luggage, we carried it, since we anticipated having to hike the ninety miles from Port Nelson to the railway and we wanted to get used to it now.

We rested only twice on the hike, when the

193

half-breeds shot ptarmigan, which now were almost completely white, signifying the rapid approach of winter.

It was desolation, this muskeg country. Stunted, burned, dying spruce poked up through the soft moss in ugly, scarlike patches. Three feet under the surface, ice exists the year around. We sank to our knees every few steps.

There was no trail; the half-breeds traveled simply by instinct. By the time we had burst out of the swamp and beheld the mighty Nelson River, eight times as large as the Hayes, one of Walt's legs was going bad. He had twisted his ankle.

In another canoe we paddled the four miles across the river, and before we reached the opposite side pelting rain hit us and huge waves billowed in from open sea. We could not paddle against the wind to the settlement of Port Nelson, so we hiked. Each step for Walt was torture. How then, were we to hike the ninety miles to the railroad? It was pitch dark and bitter cold and the storm was increasing when we reached the tiny shack maintained by the company. We pulled off our clothes and huddled before the

194

stove. I removed Walt's boot, and our spirits fell when we beheld his swollen ankle.

Port Nelson is but an abandoned heap of six million dollars worth of construction machinery. Once it was to be the railway terminal, but the project was stopped half done. A grade reaches the port, up which we had expected to hike to the railroad proper.

Factor Harding had given us letters to the mounted policemen stationed there, but as we sat before the fire, Alex Spence, one of our guides, informed us in halting English that the men were on a week's hunting trip. Walt and I were the only white persons in the place. And because of his foot, we could not set out for the railroad!

While he and I stared dumbly at each other, despairing of our next move, Alec and his partner were talking in Cree. Suddenly the half-breeds began pulling on their mukluks, motioning us to dress likewise. Into the driving rain we headed, jumping ravines and ditches until we came suddenly up against the back door of a log cabin.

Walt and I halted in the dark outer shed while our guides went into a lighted room. We could hear heavy voices talking Cree, the occasional voice of a woman and the chattering of a child. Apparently, we were not to receive a formal invitation, so we strode into the dim candlelight. A squaw sat on the littered floor, making "socks" of rabbit fur for lining moccasins. A small girl sat on the edge of a bed, playing with a ragged puppy. But it was the man who lay there, shirtless and barefoot, smoking a black pipe, who attracted our attention.

His was a big face, brown, the eyes were small and set far back. His features sloped downward, lines encircling a hawklike nose, and culminating in the most cruel mouth I have seen. His body was large and his slight movements were almost catlike. He stared at us with those half-hidden eyes, and there was no sign of the usual embarrassment of the Indian in the presence of white men. It was our eyes that lowered first.

"Colin Sinclar go up to steel tomorrow in two canoe. Maybe take you," Alec said to us. Our hearts leaped, but sank again as we saw the unchanged expression on the face of Sinclar.

Then Alec pointed to Walt's ankle and spoke in Cree to the man on the bed.

He was still looking us over. After an interminable minute, he removed his pipe from his teeth and his first word, the Cree affirmative, made our blood sing. "Eh-heh, I guess so."

## CHAPTER XVI

# END OF THE TRAIL

OUR notes describe the next few days:

"September 25. Rainy, cold. Started up Nelson in two boats, Bud in larger with Sinclar, Walt in smaller with another half-breed, Peter Masson. Made 25 miles. Sinclar shot a seal, great fat fellow. Missed another. We have terrible time keeping their boat straight with poles while they start their motors. Slept in their big tent on bed of boughs.

September 26. Up at 4:30. Current worse. Put up sails and with the motors and poling made through long shallow which they expected to track up. Raining, very cold. Sinclar says snow tomorrow! Tracked through rapids with big ropes. Hands now bleeding from the ropes. Bud ran boot nail into his heel, but we couldn't stop. Sinclar pulled out the nail. Sinclar is a tough customer, but didn't yell at us when he saw we could guide him through the rapids better than he could do it himself.

September 27. Freezing cold, snow in mid-morning. Through Limestone Rapids to railroad, at Mile 352. Just missed a freight going south. Saw its smoke. Paid men six dollars after argument. After all, without our help they wouldn't have made it so fast. Feet in bad shape. Now staying in shack of R. R. pumpman, Henry Lofgren."

And for two more nights we stayed there, while our mangled feet healed, waiting for the "Muskeg Limited" to come through from Churchill on its way south.

At Mile 327 we received a wire from Norway House and its contents took a tremendous load of worry from us, for it said that their message to Minneapolis that we were lost, had been purposely delayed a few days, and had not been sent. Evidently, the forestry men had a "hunch" that we had been merely delayed by some means and not lost.

Days later, torn, tattered, unshaved, unshorn, looking as though we came from the ends of the world, Walter and I thumped into the Winnipeg Canoe Club. They would not believe our story until we showed them our letters and other evidence. That night we were introduced, unkempt though we were, to the entire club, at a dance.

"That's what I call *some* paddling," the president said, as he told of our trip to the listening dancers.

My heart swelled with pride and happiness, and

Walt's grip on my arm grew tighter and tighter as the crowd burst into applause. I was happy because of our achievement, and so was Walter, but there was something else he was grinning about that night. For in his tattered breast pocket was a rumpled envelope, and in it was a letter informing him that "because of the nature of the circumstances" school authorities at home who were interested in him, had secured another scholarship—this time to a college in southern Illinois, where he could go that winter to begin study.

What more could we wish for?

On the eleventh of October Walter and I reached Minneapolis. We had left when the city was in the bloom of spring, buds were sprouting into new leaves and the grass was turning green, and the air was soft like rain water. As we walked toward home, our boots kicked up dead leaves that covered the sidewalks, the grass was turning into the drabness of fall, the smell of bonfires was in the sharp air, and smoke arose from the chimneys.

We went by the school, sitting on its terraces among yellow trees. As we drew nearer and nearer to home, high-school boys and girls passed us on their way to classes. We realized that we were looking at them through different eyes. We realized that our shoulders were not tired under the weight of our packs. It was as though we had suddenly become men and were boys no longer.

# INDEX

ANIMALS, seen by canoeists, 17, 19, 20, 23, 29, 45, 46, 59, 60, 64, 82, 83, 136, 164. *See also* Dogs, Wolves, Hunting

Ashton, ———, of Royal Canadian Air Force, 122, 124

Aswapiswanan Lake, 142

Aurora borealis, 92, 174

BALLANTYNE, ROBERT, author, 188

Barton, Ernest ("Jock"), Hudson's Bay Co. employee, 146–152, 153

Berens, ———, Cree chief, 96

Berens River, Man., 106, 110; canoeists at, 90–104, 108–112; Methodist mission, 94

Big Stone Lake, 3, 43; canoeists on, 32–36

Birds, seen by canoeists, 16, 41, 45, 66, 80, 164, 175. *See also* Hunting

Bloodvein River, post, 146

Blue Earth River, mouth, 22

Bois de Sioux River, reached, 38–40; canoeists on, 41–44

Browns Valley, Minn., 36

Buffington, "Tim," Winnipeg movie censor, 67

Butchart, Ralph, Hudson's Bay Co. clerk, 132–142, 145, 146

CAMPING AND CAMPSITES, equipment and methods, 11–14, 34, 81, 131, 161, 164, 168, 176, 198; experiences on trip, 26, 28–30, 32, 33, 38, 42, 45, 65–67, 73, 83, 91, 104, 156

Canada, canoeists' route, 3, 62–200; customs, 62, 64; Mounties, 92, 99, 100, 108, 118, 121, 185, 195; forest rangers, 97, 108, 118, 122; air force, 122, 124

Canoe Club, Winnipeg, 66–68, 71, 72, 73, 74, 76, 80, 90, 120, 199

Canoeing, paddling and sailing methods, 11, 28, 73, 78, 80, 87, 124, 136; effects of wilderness, 165–170. *See also* Cree Indians, "Sans Souci"

Carver, Minn., 14

Churchill, Man., 199

Clemons, ———, tug captain, 86, 106

Cowan, Herb, prospector, 70, 72, 92

Cree Indians, 100, 117; settlements, 83, 93–97, 119, 145, 146, 170; canoeists, 87, 88, 89, 125, 132, 139, 169; customs and language, 87, 141, 142, 148, 169; fur company employees, 91–95, 132–142, 152; chief, 96; fire crew, 122; church, 188. *See also* Half-breeds

Crookston, Minn., 53, 54, 55

DIVIDES, continental, 43, 124

Dogs, huskies, 90, 150, 183, 185, 186

"Donald," half-breed, 148

Drayton, N.D., pontoon bridge, 57

Durwar, Ken, pilot, 117

ECHIMAMISH RIVER, 176; name, 124; portages, 124, 128, 129, 133, 137, 138, 139, 141

Emerson, Man., customs office, 62, 64

Equipment, for trip, 8, 12, 13, 15, 20, 41, 47, 61, 134, 157, 192. *See also* Food, Guns, Maps, "Sans Souci"

Everett, Willie, Cree Indian, 91–96

FAIRMONT, N.D., 43

Fargo, N.D., 20, 47–52, 53

Fires, forest, 122, 130, 142, 153. *See also* Rangers

Fish and fishing, types of observed, 14, 17, 26, 28, 35; as canoeists' food, 23, 30, 31, 149, 163, 165; illegal, 37, 38

Food, canoeists' supplies, 9, 17–19, 23, 30, 31, 43, 44, 45, 71, 100, 118, 120, 123, 136, 151, 163, 173, 177, 183. *See also* Fish and fishing, Hunting

Fort Garry, 72

Fort Ridgely, 24

Fort Snelling, 10

"Fort York," schooner, 178, 181

French, in Canada, 63, 65

Fur trade, 61, 72; "trippers," 91, 152; trappers, 100, 110, 118, 121. *See also* Hudson's Bay Co., various posts

GODS LAKE, 120, 132, 143; canoeists on, 144–155; Elk Island, 153

Gods River, 120, 152, 153, 187; canoeists on, 155–170; portages, 121, 156, 165, 168; rapids, 121, 157–161, 170

Gordon, Walter, Hudson's Bay Co. employee, 172

Gore, Moses, Cree Indian, 132–142

Grand Forks, N.D., 54, 55

Granite Falls, Minn., 27

Gronvold, Dr. Frederick, Fargo physician, 50–52, 55

Guns, canoeists', 62, 71, 123

HAIRY LAKE, 130

Half-breeds, 112, 148; Berens River, 100; York Factory, 189; as guides, 192–197, 198

Harding, Christy, Hudson's Bay Co. factor, 180, 183; biography, 185; letters, 193, 195

Hawkes, Archie, Hudson's Bay Co. employee, 181, 190

Hayes River, 70, 121, 173, 187, 192, 194; canoeists on, 175–178

Henderson, Minn., 17

Henry, William, Hudson's Bay Co. employee, 146–149

Hudson Bay, 61, 72, 86, 106, 120, 187; canoeists' goal, 3, 5, 14, 15, 54, 65, 83, 84; canoeists at, 178–193

Hudson Bay Railway, 120, 191, 192, 193, 195, 198, 199

Hudson's Bay Co., posts, 72, 92, 100, 109, 117, 118, 132, 139, 145–152, 172, 179–193, 194; employees, 93, 132–142, 145, 146–152, 172, 180–183, 185, 188, 189, 190, 193, 195; history, 117, 179, 188

Hunting, by canoeists, 88, 90, 123, 129, 174; by Indians, 183, 194, 198

INDIANS, 55; names, 134. *See also* Cree Indians, Sioux Indians

Insects, mosquitoes, 13, 27, 39, 42, 73; flies, 31, 46, 48, 54, 60

Island Lake, mission, 126

JOHNSON, F. W., New Ulm resident, 23

Jones, Pvt. Alfred, policeman, 99, 109

KEMP, BETTY, inn owner's daughter, 100, 104, 108

Kemp, Dickie, inn owner's son, 108

Kensington, Minn., rune stone, 186

LAC QUI PARLE, 30

Lake Traverse, 15, 16, 37

Lake Winnipeg, 3, 11, 69, 70, 117, 146, 187; lighthouses, 74, 76; canoeists on, 75–113; name, 80; islands, 82, 83, 86, 87, 89, 91, 104; Cree Indians, 83, 87, 88, 89; narrows, 89; steamboats, 107, 109–113

Little Lake Traverse (Mud Lake), 38–40

Little Playgreen Lake, 122

Lofgren, Henry, railroad man, 199

Lowe, ———, inn manager, 120

McDONALD, ———, Hudson's Bay Co. employee, 181

McGill University, 110

Manitoba, bureau of mines, 69; parliament building, 69; canoeists' route, 62–200; French in, 63, 65; uncharted area, 154; muskeg, 192–194

Mankato, Minn., 14, 15, 21

Maps, canoeists' use of, 17, 69, 74, 124, 128, 137, 143, 154

Masson, Peter, guide, 198

Methodists, Berens River mission, 94

Minneapolis, Minn., 8, 14, 62, 189; Sevareid's home, 3; mayor's letter, 68; radio stations, 190; return to, 200

*Minneapolis Star,* sponsors canoe trip, 4, 5, 14, 22, 28, 34, 47, 100, 109, 119, 120, 122, 181

Minnesota River, 3, 8; canoeists on, 10–33; rapids, 14, 16, 20, 21, 26, 27; Belleview Falls, 26; portages, 26, 28

Minnesota River Valley, 24

Missions, Indian, 94, 110, 126, 188, 189

Mississippi River, 8, 23

Morton, Minn., 25

Mosquitoes. *See* Insects

Mounties. *See* Royal Canadian Mounted Police

Mud Lake, 38–40

Muskeg, in Canada, 192–194

"Muskeg Limited," railroad train, 199

NELSON RIVER, 187, 191, 192, 194; source, 114; portages, 118, 192; canoeists on, 122–124, 198; High Rock, 124; Limestone Rapids, 198
Nevins, Bob, pilot, 119
New Ulm, Minn., 23, 24
North Dakota, canoeists in, 20, 43–61
Northern lights. See Aurora borealis
Norway House, 3, 69, 71, 84, 106, 108, 113, 114, 122, 176, 191; mission, 110, 126, 189; canoeists at, 117; fur post, 117, 132, 139; wire from, 199

ORTONVILLE, Minn., 32, 34
Otter Tail River, 44

PADDLING. See Canoeing
Pembina, N.D., history, 61
Photographs, taken on trip, 15, 61, 64, 76
Pigeons, carrier, 97
Playgreen Inn, 118, 120, 121
Playgreen Lake, 69; name, 115; canoeists on, 115–117
Poles, in Red River Valley, 55–57
Pomme de Terre River, mouth, 31
Port, Walter C., 2; graduated, 7; injured, 48–52, 194; scholarships offered to, 57, 200; fights Sevareid, 166
Port Nelson, 86, 192, 193; name, 187; canoeists at, 194–197

Portaging, 133, 139. See also various lakes and rivers
Prices, 61, 66; gasoline, 89; steamboat fare, 109; food, 151, 173
Prospectors, 70, 72, 92, 110

RAILROADS. See Hudson Bay Railway
Rangers, forest, 97, 108, 118, 122
Rapids. See various rivers
Red River of the North, 3, 20, 186; source, 43, 44; rapids, 45; described, 46, 53, 65, 73; Indians on, 55
Red Sucker Creek, 163, 168
Reid, Col. ———, Hudson's Bay Co. agent, 179, 189
Robertson, James, Cree Indian, 132–142
Robertson, W. C., newspaperman, 4, 181
Robinson Lake, 138
Royal Canadian Air Force, 122, 124
Royal Canadian Mounted Police, 92, 99, 100, 108, 118, 121, 185, 195
Rune stone, Kensington, 186
Russell, Alec, farmer, 24

ST. ANDREWS DAM, 72
St. Jean, Man., 65
St. Peter, Minn., 20
Sandy River, Man., Cree settlement, 83
"Sans Souci," canoe named and described, 5, 8; lost, 16; damaged, 37, 165, 174; towed, 43; customs charge, 62; shipped, 109; abandoned, 192. See also Canoeing

205

Scots, in fur trade, 61, 135
Seaplanes, 98, 116; pilots, 106, 117, 119
Selkirk, Man., 71, 72
Seton, Ernest Thompson, naturalist, 185
Sevareid, Arnold Eric, high school career, 3, 6; *Minneapolis Star* stories, 14, 22, 28, 34, 100, 119; injured, 30, 198; family, 32, 50, 53; fights Port, 166
Severn River, 189; post, 181
Shakopee, Minn., 14; name, 15
Shamattawa River, 167; Indian settlement, 163, 170; canoeists on, 170–175; post, 172; rapids, 172, 174; name, 173
Shepherd, ———, steamboat purser, 109
Sherman, Karl, trapper, 121, 127, 154, 163
Sinclair, Colin, Cree Indian, 196–199
Sioux Indians, 15, 24
Skull Island, 147
Solomon, Cree Indian, 152
South Dakota, 3, 33
Southern, Sam, club caretaker, 67
Spence, Alex, guide, 195
Steamboats, 120; at New Ulm, 23; Red River Channel, 74; at Berens River, 94, 97; on Lake Winnipeg, 107, 109–113
Stefansson, Vilhjalmur, explorer, 185
Stewart, Cpl. Hugh, policeman, 99, 102
Sucker Creek, rapids, 121

THIRD, JOCK, trader, 172, 174

Touchwood Lake, 142; described, 143
Trees, types of observed, 44, 79, 81, 93, 130, 137, 155, 170, 194
Trout, Joe, "medicine man," 148

UNIVERSITY OF CHICAGO, 57, 191

VICTORIA BEACH, MAN., 80–82

WAGES, for fire fighting, 122; for guides, 198
Wahpeton, N.D., 44
Walters, Rev. ———, missionary, 110
Warren Landing, Man., 113, 114
Water, canoeists' supply, 11, 31, 38
Watkins, Bill, ranger, 122
Weather, hot, 11, 25, 32, 38; rain, fog, and hail, 13, 26, 29, 33, 47, 115, 143, 156–162, 174, 194, 198; cold, 43, 52, 59, 87, 131, 164; windy, 85, 87, 102, 105–108, 115, 143; snow, 198
Whetstone Creek, 33
Winnipeg, Man., 47, 98, 110, 120, 148; canoeists at, 64–71; mayor, 68; newspapers, 180
Winnipeg Beach, Man., 73
"Wolverine," steamboat, 107, 109–113
Wolves, 89, 164

YELLOW MEDICINE RIVER, mouth, 27
York boat, 118
York Factory, fur post, 106, 109, 118, 120, 122, 131, 152, 154, 173, 174, 177; mission, 110, 188; canoeists at, 179–193